COLORADO

ROADSIDE PHOTOGRAPHY GUIDE

TEXT BY ROBERT L. CASTELLINO
PHOTOGRAPHY BY ROBERT L. CASTELLINO
& LEN KRUEGER

D1410910

SPECIAL THANKS

The following people have made this book possible. To each one of them a special thank you is extended for their interest, influence and effort to ensure its accuracy.

The Rocky Mountain Association of Geologists – Jack Rathbone, Sandy Pellissier, Bruce Kelso

Larry Fredrick, Chief of Interpretation, Rocky Mountain National Park

Jim Kavitz, Interpretational Director, Aspen Center for Environmental Studies

David Whitman, Chief of Interpretation, Dinosaur National Monument

Ron Young, Chief of Interpretation, Colorado National Monument

Sally Crum, Forester and Interpreter, Grand Mesa National Forest

Liane Mattson, Forester and Interpreter, Grand Mesa National Forest

Kyle Patterson, Park Information Officer, Black Canyon of the Gunnison National Park

Linda Martin, Interpreter, Mesa Verde National Park

Carol Sperling, Chief of Interpretation, Great Sand Dunes National Monument and Preserve

Copyright © 2003 Robert L. Castellino, Photographer and Author

Text: Robert L. Castellino

Photography: Robert L. Castellino and Len Krueger

Editor: Carmel Huestis

Illustrations & Calligraphy: Charmayne Bernhardt

Creative Director and Publisher: Robert L. Castellino

Designer: Len Krueger

Maps: www.colorado.com

All rights reserved. No part of this book may be reproduced in any form or by any electronic or mechanical means, information storage and retrieval systems, without permission in writing from the publisher, except by a reviewer who may quote brief passages in reviews.

Whispering River, LLC
Louisville, Colorado
Phone: 720-890-8655
www.whisperingriver.com

Printed and Bound in China
Through Kaliedo Graphic Services Group, Inc.

ISBN 1-879914-86-7 (Soft Cover)

First Printing 2003

CONTENTS

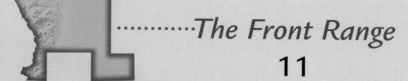

Introduction

The road to the heart of Colorado begins wherever you start your journey. The end of the road leads you to countless places of amazing beauty in Colorado. Along the way you may find more wonders than you anticipated and a few you never imagined existed. Across the state, through the change of seasons, from morning until the last light of day, someplace, somewhere, an inspired moment occurs in which an exceptional photograph is waiting to be made. All it takes is getting out on the road to find these places. Making photographs as you travel creates opportunities to learn about Colorado's diverse landscape, natural phenomena, Western history, geology, Native people, ecology, wildlife and contemporary culture. It's been said, "It may take a lifetime to see Colorado, and as many years to learn about everything she has to offer." A Colorado photographic excursion is a ride worth repeating over and over again—and it may take several trips to get the picture you came to make.

Start with any one of the locations found in these pages. You may have been to some already and want to return again. This photography guide has been organized to highlight some of the most noted places, some unknown treasures, and the routes to get you there. A map of Colorado dividing the state into seven geographic regions makes planning your photographic excursions easy. You are guided counterclockwise around the state from the Front Range, to the Northwest, the Southwest to South Central, north to Denver, then back to the Northeast and ending in the Southeast. You may choose one destination or link a series in a geographic region for an extended trip.

The focus of the guide is an easy approach to the art of making extraordinary photographs in the field. There are directions to most of the locations to help you find them, and perspectives of the exceptional views and vistas to be found there. Knowledge of how to use your camera is critical in making masterfully crafted photographs, so the first step is to learn how your camera operates and know its full range of functions. Knowing your camera is the basis for developing technique and style. The fundamental elements and components found in working and extraordinary photographs are described at the beginning of the guide. As you turn each page, you will find "PhotoTips" on how the photographs were made, and specific tips on how to approach each setting and situation. If you care to dig a little deeper, you will find why photographers are drawn to these places. You will begin to understand that making a photograph is a good excuse to hit the road so you can uncover the story that connects the place to the picture.

Set your worldly cares aside and ride out to any place in the state. Drive to the end of the road that appears to lead nowhere in particular. Turn down one of the many scenic byways or country roads to see where it leads. Maybe you prefer a day in one of Colorado's Western towns or resorts or the excitement of a Denver happening. If you're weary of driving, have had it with crowds in the city or on the beaten path, take a quiet walk or hike in the backcountry.

There is more to Colorado than the grand expanse though. Just look a little closer through your camera's viewfinder with a macro lens. Get up close. Lay down in a field of wildflowers in a high mountain meadow or seek out the light dancing across the crest of waves on a rushing river. Watch the sandhill cranes at the Monte Vista Wildlife Refuge or the elk rutting in Rocky Mountain National Park. There are hundreds of great escapes on Bureau of Land Management (BLM) lands. You might be lucky enough to track wild horses running free on the range near the Book Cliffs north of Grand Junction.

Let your impulses run with the wind. Follow your heart's desire into the endless possibilities of Colorado. You won't be disappointed. There are thousands of photographs, stories and adventures waiting for you at every turn.

The Art of Making Photographs

Often the theory and science of photography are explained in painstaking detail, confusing all but masters of the craft. Unfortunately, for those of us who want to pick up a camera and expect our results to match those of the masters in fine art photography, the pleasure of making a photograph is lost in technical terms when we are trying to learn how to use our camera. Fortunately, for those who are using a camera for the first time, or for those who carry a camera with them wherever they go, there is a set of fundamental rules that can make the art of photography easier. This guide is designed to help you create, make and identify photographs for your album or files like professionals do.

Photography is an art. It is a craft that requires practice, dedication and learning—experimenting with different techniques—a process of trial and error. Until recently, using traditional manual 35mm cameras took understanding the complex operations of the camera, and it also took a fair amount of skill to create consistent images. The development of "point and shoot" cameras programmed to meter light while managing aperture settings and shutter speeds made photography more accessible to more people. Autofocus zoom lenses revolutionized camera equipment. The only complication was waiting for the film to be processed to discover if any of the photographs accurately captured the special image seen through the viewfinder. Today, digital cameras have made it easier than ever to review a photograph, determine its imperfections, and replace the photo with a new one—just as fast as you made and erased the first. Without further concern for equipment, let's review a series of steps that make the art of photography simpler.

Photographs can be categorized as records: ones that work, ones that are exceptional or extraordinary. A record is a crisply focused photograph capturing a moment, a person, a place or subject, yet lacks color, imagination in composition, and beautiful light. It may also be filled with distracting elements of clutter and lines of confusion that move the viewer's eye away from the subject—where it truly belongs. Working photographs demonstrate the photographer's ability to balance composition, light and color to define and complement the subject of the photograph. The viewer sees the subject as it was found, yet the image—although stirring—misses the mark in defining the moment as profound and beyond the ordinary. Elements of exceptional or extraordinary photographs are made of a single subject, a simple idea, and speak volumes about the photographer behind the lens. The drama is compelling and evocative. These photos cause us to stop, pause and contemplate in awe before moving on. The photographer has taken the time to define, compose and expose the subject to the camera, graphically defining what he or she intends to convey in its final printed form. The photographer, not the photograph, holds us in check and in wonder. We ask, "How, why and what was going on in that enlightening moment?"

Planning Your Photographs

1) Research and study the location– Take the time to study a specific photographic subject or location. Give yourself sufficient time to understand the subtle nuances of each location, and plan to visit the location at least three times.

2) Set Up– Be sure to place and secure your tripod then fasten your camera on the tripod to assure it will not vibrate when releasing the shutter. Consider your options of photographing the scene from all angles and moving while the light is good. Look 360 degrees from where you set up. You may find if the light is great on the subject you have chosen, it may be even better in other directions from the same place.

3) Compose– Choose the focal length lens or zoom to the focal length you desire. Look through the viewfinder and study perspective from top to bottom, side to side, corner to corner and in each quadrant. Make sure you have the subject, and everything you desire, in sharp focus. Eliminate lines of distraction and clutter. Back away and look at the scene from behind the camera again. Then look through the viewfinder once again. Repeat these steps, confirming this is the photograph that you intend to make.

4) Expose– Unless you rely on your camera's automatic features, we recommend that you set your exposures manually to assure you achieve the desired result. Low available first or last light requires setting your aperture at its greatest value (f22 or f32) or smallest opening. Slower shutter speeds are known to increase the depth of field, exposing more detail for landscape photos. Make sure you have set the ISO to the value recommended by the film manufacturer or as desired with a digital camera. Use a slow speed ISO film of 50 to increase saturation and color for landscapes and still life photographs. High speed ISO films of 100, 200, 400, 800, or even 1600

allow you to stop action in higher light, including wildlife and sports subjects, where you would use faster shutter speeds and smaller aperture values (f4.5 or f2.0). Note that advanced digital cameras adjust to the setting automatically, unless you override them manually—even to the extent of setting the ISO, shutter speed and aperture. Once you have determined the exposure value, you are ready to make the long-awaited photo.

5) Wait– After you have followed these preliminary steps, the key to making extra-ordinary photographs is waiting—until your visual senses are tuned and attentive to the light and the action. Your subject may be a small waterfall with mountains in the background, when you realize that a bighorn sheep is waltzing through your view-finder, or clouds clear with a shaft of light perfectly backlighting the leaves or grass. Magical moments like these are why we go back, many times, to make a photograph of a place or setting.

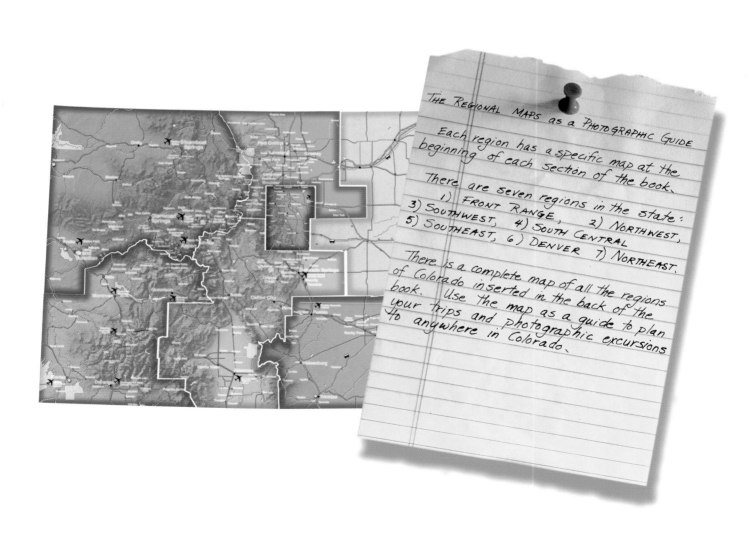

THE REGIONAL MAPS as a PHOTOGRAPHIC GUIDE

Each region has a specific map at the beginning of each section of the book.

There are seven regions in the state: 1) FRONT RANGE, 2) NORTHWEST, 3) SOUTHWEST, 4) SOUTH CENTRAL 5) SOUTHEAST, 6) DENVER 7) NORTHEAST.

There is a complete map of all the regions of Colorado inserted in the back of the book. Use the map as a guide to plan your trips and photographic excursions to anywhere in Colorado.

Dream Lake

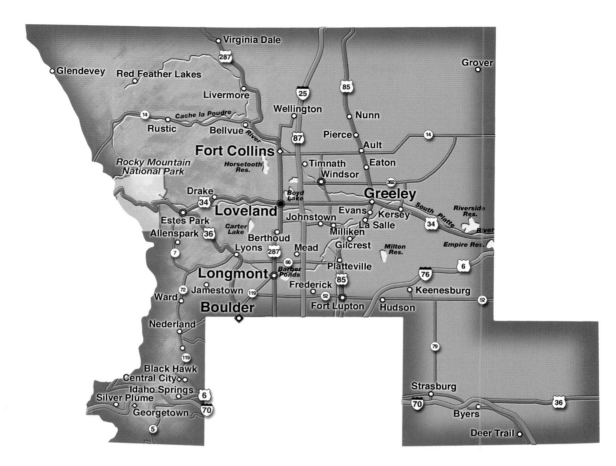

THE
Front Range
R E G I O N

The Front Range Region encompasses some of Colorado's most noted landmarks and treasures. The landscape is dramatic from plains to rolling foothills and skyward to the snow-capped peaks of the Rockies. It's a safe bet to start your photographic journey in and along the Front Range. Rocky Mountain National Park, Colorado's crown jewel, boasts Trail Ridge Road, the highest continuous road in the contiguous lower 48 states. The highest road in America winds to the top of 14,000-foot Mount Evans from the storied mining town of Idaho Springs. The monolithic sandstone Flatirons seen from every corner of

2 **Last light–the Eldorado Springs water gap**

Boulder define the "Front Range." The historic Peak to Peak Scenic Byway stretches from Estes Park to Central City and Blackhawk, offering grand vistas and escapes into the Indian Peaks Wilderness.

The changing seasons play an important part in the beauty of the Front Range, as much as the elevation does, climbing from just over 5,000 feet on the plains to 14,000

3 **Dall Sheep– Mount Evans**

feet on Longs Peak, Mount Bierstadt and Mount Evans. Wildlife is abundant in the open spaces and mountain parks. You might be surprised at the range, variety and number of wild creatures found right in the backyards of urban Colorado. Keep your eye on the lookout as you head down the road to any one of the places we suggest you visit.

4 Sunrise from East Boulder wetlands

5 Flatirons—view from Marshall Mesa

Boulder County

Native Culture and Early Development

Boulder County is the home of the University of Colorado, Pearl Street and the majestic Flatirons. Boulder's historical roots are preserved in the local architecture and reflected by the Flatirons and the thousands of acres of open space. In the 1850s, during the gold rush, settlers arrived seeking their fortunes. They founded Boulder City, which became a mining supply town named after the jumble of large rocks at the mouth of the nearby canyon. Not too many years after it was founded, Boulder City became Boulder, and the name change stuck. The local Arapaho and Cheyenne tribes were relocated from their land; however, many of the nearby peaks, canyons and city streets were named in tribute to the Native cultural heritage: Left Hand Canyon, Arapahoe Avenue, Niwot Ridge and more. The boomtown floundered with the bust of the gold rush and later the crash of the silver market in 1893. Yet Boulder was bolstered by the state legislature granting it the right to build the University of Colorado, and Old Main, its first structure, opened for classes in the fall of 1877. The University of Colorado campus is the predominant feature of the city scape, and, during the academic year the university adds more than 25,000 students and more than 8,000 faculty and staff members to the local population. The sandstone architecture and terracotta roofs, modeled on those found in Italy's Tuscan region, make CU one of the most recognizable campuses in the United States.

6 **Barn and Silo– Arapahoe Road**

Central to downtown is the illustrious Pearl Street Mall, a revitalization project completed in 1977. Pearl Street was named after the shaft of late afternoon light that extends from west to east along the canyon walls and down the street, illuminating everything along the way like a string of pearls. Pearl Street is a center of activity for visitors from around the world. People watching, shopping and a variety of sidewalk entertainers make Pearl Street one of the more popular outdoor walking malls in Colorado.

The Flatirons or Fountain Formation

More than 100 million years ago, dunes and beaches were formed as seas encroached from the north and south, then receded. Worked by the sea over centuries, the dunes

7 **Green Mountain Cabin–Flagstaff Mountain**

and beaches turned to brittle sandstone. These layers of sedimentary rock tipped at a 50-degree angle, creating the Fountain

8 **Continental Divide from Artist Point**

Formation (the Flatirons) and the Dakota Formation (Echo Rock) along a faultline running north and south. Streams formed by rain and snowmelt from glaciers carved deep V-shaped canyons where South Boulder, Bear and Boulder Creeks run today. Alluvial fans of glacial debris formed terraces and outwashed plains to the east.

The Rest of the Boulder Story

Many fabled characters have left their mark on Boulder. Among them are photographer Joseph B. Sturdevant, alias Rocky Mountain Joe; Chief Niwot, or Left Hand, a legendary, multilingual Arapaho chief who met the first

10 **Juggler on the Pearl Street Mall**

Anglo settlers; Mary Rippon, the quirky CU professor whose name graces the amphitheatre where the Colorado Shakespeare Festival makes its home; and Allen Ginsberg, the rebellious and irreverent poet of the 1950s and 1960s.

Chautauqua Park, at the entrance to Boulder's Mountain Parks, was originally established in the early 1890s as Texado Park by a group of Texas schoolteachers, performing and visual artists and outdoor enthusiasts seeking the cooler summer climate of Colorado as a respite from the Texas heat. When the Chautauqua movement swept across the country, developing regional

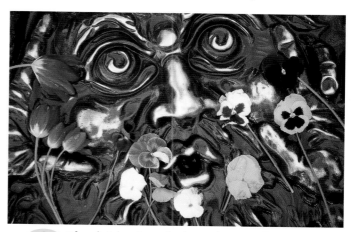

9 **Blowin' in the wind on the Pearl Street Mall**

centers of theatrical study, education, and the arts, the name was changed. Today this historical landmark is well preserved with cabins, auditorium, administrative building, lodges and dining hall. The park still offers everything its founders had envisioned—and more—through a wide variety of city-run performances, programs and activities. Having a picnic and enjoying an evening concert at the park is one of Boulder's favorite summer outings.

Boulder is notorious for its independent, free-spirited character and its attitude as the universal center of everything. There are more than a few good jokes about Boulder—the most famous may be "Boulder is 28 miles of open space surrounded by reality." All jokes

11 **Winter Flatirons–Chautauqua Park**

aside, Boulder is considered one of the most livable cities in the country. The quality of life that Boulder provides is supported by living close to nature and by the conservation efforts to limit growth and acquire open space. Boulder's beauty and easy access make photographing this place a breeze.

Where to Photograph in Boulder

Here are few suggestions on where to go and when to get the best conditions. Travel over to Walden Ponds, east of Boulder, for a variety of wildlife. Hike into the Flatirons and Boulder's Mountain Parks for nature. Watch the sun rise at the meadow below the Flatirons in Chautauqua Park. Or take a late afternoon/evening stroll on the Pearl Street Mall or along Boulder Creek near Settlers Park. To capture the most beautiful light, mornings are best for westward views of the Flatirons and from atop Flagstaff Mountain at Artist's Point for views of the

Continental Divide. Evenings offer the best eastward perspectives for places like the Pearl Street Mall and parts of the University of Colorado Campus. Atmospheric conditions play a major role in this area, especially in places like Chautauqua Park where you find people at play in the afternoons and the wetlands on the east edge of town. If you are looking for activities and people, visit the Pearl Street Mall at twilight or after dark. You are guaranteed to find a crowd on the Pearl Street Mall almost every night throughout the summer.

Photography Tip: Plan your locations based on the time of day to capture the warm available light for each shoot. Look for opportunities where people are naturally having fun.

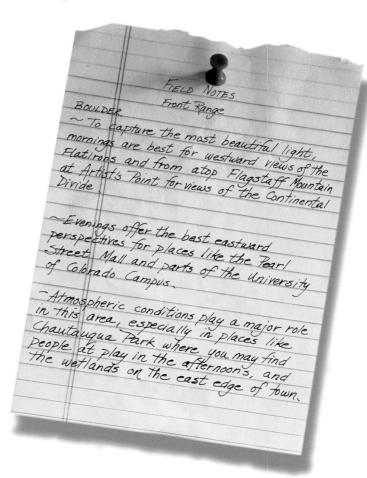

FIELD NOTES
Front Range

BOULDER
~ To capture the most beautiful light, mornings are best for westward views of the Flatirons and from atop Flagstaff Mountain at Artist's Point for views of the Continental Divide.

~Evenings offer the best eastward perspectives for places like the Pearl Street Mall and parts of the University of Colorado Campus.

~Atmospheric conditions play a major role in this area, especially in places like Chautauqua Park where you may find people at play in the afternoons, and the wetlands on the east edge of town.

12) Fall–Bierstadt Lake Trail

Rocky Mountain National Park

Colorado's Legendary Park

The name itself is legendary: "Rocky Mountain National Park." The voices that created this place echo through National Park lore as if they could be heard from peak to peak across the Park's valleys. As the word "epic" describes a series of single, extraordinary life-changing events, one

visit to Rocky Mountain National Park can, in a flash, transform your perception of its power. Or, it may take a lifetime of many visits to fully comprehend its grandeur.

The terrain is expansive: 416 square miles. The geography is rugged—the top of Longs Peak extends to 14,259 feet, and the nearby town of Estes Park rests at an elevation

13) First snow–Bear Lake

of 7,522 feet above sea level. The geology is fascinating and the wildlife is abundant; both are visually accessible from the roadway that traverses through the Park. Even with more than a million visitors each year, much of Rocky Mountain National Park remains as it was when it was founded—untouched and wild.

14 **Nymph Lake at sunset**

About 300 million years ago, the "Ancestral Rockies" were uplifted, then worn completely away over the course of 200 million years through a period known as the Cambrian Age.

A sea encroached from the north and south during the Cretaceous period about

15 **Lenticular clouds at sunset near Longs Peak**

Were it not for the founder's prudent efforts to preserve it for generations to come, this magnificent Colorado treasure may have been another over-developed theme park. Once you experience Rocky Mountain National Park, you know that you can't take it for granted.

The Rocky Mountain Geology

Before the first uplift of the Rockies nearly 550 million years ago, a break in the rock record occurred, and this stratigraphic column is known as the "Great Uncomformity." Rock formations created before this period are known as Precambrian.

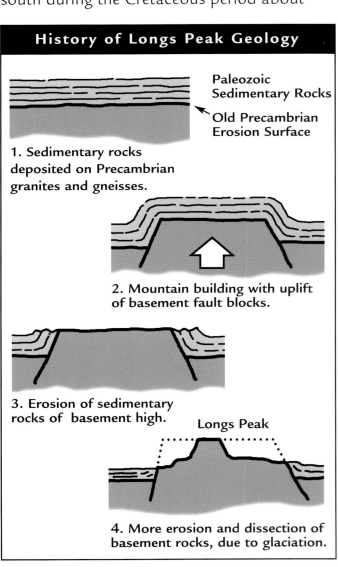

History of Longs Peak Geology

Paleozoic Sedimentary Rocks

Old Precambrian Erosion Surface

1. Sedimentary rocks deposited on Precambrian granites and gneisses.

2. Mountain building with uplift of basement fault blocks.

3. Erosion of sedimentary rocks of basement high.

Longs Peak

4. More erosion and dissection of basement rocks, due to glaciation.

16 **Rock gap on Trail Ridge Road**

100 million years ago. Dinosaurs thrived, then vanished. Some 65 million years ago the present-day Rocky Mountains began to form during the Tertiary Period. Sediments laid down in the Cretaceous sea were pushed skyward, then eroded, exposing the Precambrian rocks that are the core of today's Rocky Mountains. The uplifts came in waves or pulses and combined with igneous intrusions, volcanic eruptions and mountain building, ultimately producing the grand mountains we see today. Glaciers carved deep valleys and sculpted the steep canyon walls, steps, bowls and wide valley floors where rivers run and lakes exist now. Even though the continuous glacial process of erosion started a million years ago and came to a close just 10,000 years ago, water and ice are still at work today, but not quite as actively as before.

Native Culture and Settlers

The abundance of animals and plants attracted Native Americans to the Park for several thousand years. The Ute are known as the "mountain people" as they have been in the mountains of Colorado for at least 6,000 years. Early Apache groups entered the area in the 1500s, and the Arapaho in the early 1800s. Native peoples were removed

Abert's Squirrel

17 **Glacier Creek near Bear Lake Road**

to reservations by the 1850s, as the area began to be occupied first by miners and ranchers, and later with lodges and resorts in

Big Horn Sheep

the Grand Lake and Estes Park areas.

Many legendary characters left their marks on this region since the first Anglo settlers made their way here. Among them are Major Stephen H. Long (whose name was given to the peak on the southeast section of the Park), settler Joel Estes (after whom Estes Park was named), John Wesley Powell (explorer) and William Byers (the first Anglo to climb Longs Peak). English explorer and author Isabella Bird (author of *A Lady's Life in the Rocky Mountains*), Frederick Chapin (author of *Mountaineering in Colorado*), Albert Bierstadt (the great 1800s landscape painter) and the ingenious F. O. Stanley (the co-inventor of the Stanley Steamer automobile and builder

18 Bristlecone Pines near Trail Ridge Road

determined to see these wild lands preserved and not stripped of their beauty for the economic value of their minerals, timber and water rights. Through his efforts and those of many others, Rocky Mountain National Park came into existence with the stroke of President Woodrow Wilson's pen on January 26, 1915. Mills's dream made it possible for us today to share his love of the land almost as he found it.

of the Stanley Hotel) are all part of the area's fascinating history.

Yet it is Enos Mills, a devoted naturalist and author, who stands as a giant among this list of eminent pioneers. He was the first to propose that this pristine land be designated as the nation's tenth national park; ultimately his efforts led to the establishment of Rocky Mountain National Park. He was

Photographing Rocky Mountain National Park

Photographing the Park can be done from the edge of the road, but it's best if you take time to move out into the Park on walks and hikes. Study each valley, mountain, lake, tributary, forest and meadow to understand how the light plays and learn to see these places from

PHOTOGRAPHING the ROCKY MOUNTAIN NATIONAL PARK

~ Plan your locations based on the time of day to capture the best light for each shoot.

~ Photographing wildlife close up demands stillness, quiet and long lenses – 400mm in focal length or longer.

~ Work tenaciously, not knowing what you might find, but knowing that it is better to be out there, ready to photograph, than not going at all and wondering what you might have missed.

~ It may take returning to the Park many times to capture a few extraordinary photographs that truly define the magnificence of Rocky Mountain National Park. Each visit is a lesson that is worth the preparation and effort that inspires you to make the journey.

19 Frosted leaves

the photographer's perspective. First morning light at Alberta Falls or Moraine Park and last light at Bear or Nymph Lake will produce significant results. It takes observing with a keen eye to know the path that the local wildlife will travel and to understand nature's intricate patterns well enough to

20 **Elk grazing near Trail Ridge Road**

capture the essence of their existence. Photographing wildlife demands stillness, quiet and long lenses—400mm in focal length or longer. Wait for that special moment—perhaps watching a cow elk lead her calf to water and, with a gentle nudge, encourage it to drink. Watch the clouds retracting from the mountaintops after a thunderstorm at sunset. Experience the warm alpenglow that graces the landscape and wait for the right moment to capture this beautiful image on film. Scramble up a mountainside, and, as the moon rises into the night sky and illuminates the winding ribbon of car lights along Trail Ridge Road, allow your long, time-lapsed exposure to create an image that carefully divides the tundra in half. Go into the

foggy mist that is beginning to shroud the evening, after an early fall snowstorm, to see the glowing red and yellow leaves of a solitary aspen tree, struggling to survive in a rugged boulder field on Bear Lake Road. Learn to study the scene, to move quickly and to compose the photograph. Try adjusting the aperture to its smallest setting and the shutter speed to its slowest speed, increasing the saturation of color and depth of field, allowing you to capture this

Bald Eagle

22

21 **Aspen in rock garden near Bear Lake Road**

magical moment. Experiment by adjusting the f-stop one stop larger and, again, one stop smaller in value, in comparison to the camera's preferred meter reading, and determine which setting has created the best photograph. This is known as bracketing. Work tenaciously, not knowing what you might find, but knowing that it is better to be out there, ready to photograph, than not going at all and wondering what you might have missed. If you are visiting for a short time, trust your intuition where to set up or obtain guidance from a Park ranger as to where to start.

22 **Blue Columbine**

Begin someplace by stopping and looking through your viewfinder long enough for all of this beauty to unfold before you. Make your first photograph, then another, and before you know it, half the day is behind you. It may take returning to the Park many times to capture a few extraordinary photographs that truly define the magnificence of Rocky Mountain National Park. Each visit is a lesson that is worth the preparation and effort that inspires you to make the journey.

23 Lake Isabelle drainage

Indian Peaks Wilderness Area

Wilderness for the Ages

The drive along the Peak to Peak Scenic Byway from Estes Park to Black Hawk and Central City offers exceptional views of high peaks and extensive tracts of pine forests mixed with large groves of aspen. Popular attractions along this route include Golden

24 **Summer cascade–Pawnee Pass**

Gate Canyon State Park, Arapaho and Roosevelt National Forests and Eldora Ski Area. Yet one area along this 55-mile stretch of road separates it from all the others—Indian Peaks Wilderness. Established by Congress in 1978 the Indian Peaks Wilderness covers 76,486 acres of beautiful, pristine alpine terrain. The wilderness stretches 16 miles south from the border of Rocky Mountain National Park along the rugged

ridgeline of the Continental Divide. Indian Peaks takes its name from the nine peaks within the wilderness boundaries that were named for Native American tribes. It boasts more than 50 lakes, as many streams and more than 100 miles of hiking trails. The most often-visited wilderness in the United States, Indian Peaks Wilderness is a part of those western lands set aside to preserve their natural wonders for future generations.

> **Wilderness:** "*An area where the earth and its community of life are untrammeled by man, where man himself is a visitor who does not remain ... an area protected and managed so as to preserve its natural conditions.*"
> —The Wilderness Act of 1964

Native Americans and Pioneers

With the Indian Peaks so close to Rocky Mountain National Park, you might think the history of the ancient peoples would be the same, but that's not exactly so. Although ancient Paleo Indians may have appeared here about 9,000 years ago as in Rocky Mountain National Park, the Indian Peaks area was considered to be an important transmountain travel route up until the earliest explorers and settlers came to Colorado. Many artifacts (stone tools, pottery and campsites) have been scientifically carbon dated, validating the

Native cultures' presence. Arapaho had summered in the wilderness area hunting game. Remnants of their low rock walls, cairn lines and circular shelters used for trapping game can still be found today. This changed abruptly as the gold rush of 1859 brought miners and settlers working the earth in the quest for riches. Evidence of mining activity can be found throughout the wilderness on some of the most rugged, out-of-the-way cirques and valleys. The Fourth of July mineshaft lies near Arapaho Pass just outside the old town of Eldora. The "rush to riches," as it is known throughout Colorado, was short-lived as prospectors found only a few veins of silver or gold living up to the exaggerated rumors that spread eastward to start the rush. The exploitation of this resource-rich region was halted by a few far-sighted men, most noteworthy Enos Mills, and later Roger Toll, Rocky Mountain Park Superintendent from 1921 to 1929. Toll's efforts to annex the area known today as Indian Peaks Wilderness into the park boundary were thwarted. However, in the long run, they were not in vain, as many others years later led the charge in 1971 to introduce a bill in Congress for the Indian Peaks to become a wilderness area.

Wilderness Habitat and Wildlife

There are three climate zones in the Indian

25 **Sunrise reflection–Lake Isabelle**

Peaks Wilderness: montane at 9,000 feet, subalpine between 9,000 and 11,500 feet, and alpine above 11,500. Timberline is around 11,500. Within these zones there is a distinct set of plants and animals. The montane zone often is identified with ponds built by beaver or willow carrs. Along with beaver, a variety of birds thrive here including the American robin, Wilson's warbler, broad-tailed hummingbird and warbling vireo. Mule deer browse on plants in the carrs as cottontail and snowshoe rabbits hide among the willow. Lodgepole pine and aspen line the ponds; wildflowers, such as paintbrush, columbine and shooting stars, are common in this zone. The subalpine zone receives the greatest amount of snow, and Englemann spruce have a stronghold. Elk can be seen grazing in open meadows most often in the early morning and late evening, bear forage on small bush fruits and dig for grubs under rotting fallen trees. Birds such as the white-crowned sparrow and dark-eyed junco make their nests here during the summer months. You will find monkshood, glacier lilies and daisies in abundance. The alpine zone is most fragile because of

Pika

26 High divide above Lake Isabelle

the cold intense winds and short growing season. Everything appears to struggle for survival at this altitude; flowers such as fairy primrose, moss campion, marigold and white marsh pop in bright colors and retreat nearly as fast as they blossom. You can hear the high squeal of the pika and the call of the marmot across boulder fields, warning other rodents of your coming. If you are lucky, you might sight a white tailed ptarmigan, highly camouflaged in its seasonal colors and golden eagles soaring above the ridges looking for pika.

Geology and Geography

Indian Peaks Wilderness geologic features are similar to those found in Rocky Mountain National Park and mirror its geologic history. The formations of the rugged ridgeline create a unique skyline as seen from the plains. Mountain valleys have been scoured by glaciers whose ancestral remnants are seen under Arapaho Peak and above Lake Isabelle. The peaks are named Ogalla Peak (13,333 feet), Paiute Peak (13,083 feet), Pawnee Peak (12,939 feet), Shoshoni Peak (12,962 feet), Apache Peak (13,438 feet), Navajo Peak (13,405 feet), Arikaree Peak (12,146 feet), Arapaho Peak (13,393 feet) and Niwot Ridge. There are four trail passes leading over the divide west to east: Devil's Thumb (11,747 feet), Arapaho (11,906 feet), Pawnee (12,541 feet) and Buchanan (11, 837 feet).

27 Glacial runoff below Niwot Ridge

Photographing the Indian Peaks Wilderness

The area of concentration for photography in the Indian Peaks Wilderness is found above Brainard Lake a few miles off the road above the historic mining town of Ward, and on Arapaho Pass above Fourth of July Campground west of the town of Eldora. The roads to these locations are paved or dirt in good condition for safe passage in two-wheel-drive vehicles. Many beautiful areas of access into the wilderness yield equally exquisite results depending on the time of year. Summer is recommended for weather, color and ease of moving about by foot into the backcountry. Anytime you are photographing in the Indian Peaks from the east side (plains to mountains side) of the divide, the best light is first morning sunrise or storm light. If you are on the west side (Grand Lake or

Winter Park side) of the divide, the evenings and sunset will produce the most spectacular results. Yet never set your camera aside just because you are on the east side at sunset or on the west side at sunrise. Getting an early

28 **Sunset–Lake Thoraden**

start by hiking to your location well before sunup or sundown (often hours ahead) will give you time to reconnoiter the landscape, and set up for your shoot once you have arrived. If the light is amazing and you are photographing the subject lit with the sun behind you, don't hesitate turning 360 degrees to see what else might be of interest. Simply recompose your shot and begin shooting again. Oftentimes what you see as the subject of interest may not be the subject of interest at all.

PHOTOGRAPHING the INDIAN PEAKS WILDERNESS
~ If the light is as amazing as it is and you are photographing the subject lit with the sun behind you, don't hesitate turning 360 degrees to see what else might be of interest. Simply recompose your shot and begin shooting again. Initially what you have trained your eye on as the subject of interest may not be the subject of interest at all.

Maroon Bells

THE Northwest REGION

The most popular destinations in the Northwest Region are easiest to reach on the main thoroughfares. Along the I-70 corridor you will find Summit County, Vail, Glenwood Springs and Grand Junction. Then a bit farther down the way you will find Steamboat to the north by west, and Aspen south by central. These world-class resorts offer opportunities sought by the rich and famous, and stand at the edge of Colorado's exquisite monuments and wilderness areas—no less than the Colorado National Monument, and the Mount Zirkel and the Maroon Bells-Snowmass

30 Trappers Lake—The Flat Tops

Wildernesses. If your wanderlust heart moves you, then traverse the state by starting in the far-off reaches of the Northwest Region. You'll find places like the quiet hamlet of Maybell, the old train depot and ranching town of Phippsburg, the crossroads at Dinosaur and

31 **Fisherman-Crystal River**

33 **Bucking bronco-Steamboat Rodeo**

the sleepy tree-lined river-valley supply town of Buford, to name a few. The Northwest is where the backcountry roads of Colorado lead to the magnificent expanse of the real Wild West. Out here legends of the Old West live as testaments to the free spirit of

34 **Waterfall at Hanging Lake**

the mountain men and the last vestiges of open range. Wild in the West is defined not by what has been tamed and settled, but by what remains as it has always been—wind-

32 **Backlit broad leaf**

blown, unbridled and boundless. On a country road you feel the grit needed for rustic living in its simplicity.

Look no further to bed down on the ground under star-bright nights in the great wide open, to find where rivers run into isolated desert canyons sculpted by the elements through the eons, or walk under skies that stretch forever to the end of the rolling plateaus. Pack your camera bag, and drive on. You will not be disappointed or lack for photo opportunities.

35 **Snowstorm at Hanging Lake**

36 **Fall reflection of Maroon Lake**

Maroon Bells-Snowmass Wilderness

Reflecting on Maroon Lake

The drive up Maroon Creek Road is enough to leave you gasping in sheer amazement at the beauty of this high alpine hanging valley. Nothing may ever compare to your first sight of the reflection of Maroon Bells Peaks on Maroon Lake at sunrise. The symmetry of the mountain walls forming the lake basin is perfection. Add the backdrop of North and South Maroon Bells Peaks with beavers slapping the lake's surface in warning of your presence, and you'll know you have arrived at the Maroon Bells-Snowmass Wilderness. This is true wilderness as defined by the Wilderness Act of 1964, nothing less—the grand

37 **South shore on Maroon Lake**

cathedral entrance of all entrances to a wilderness area. Far and away, this is the most photographed, and the most recognizable, Colorado Rocky Mountain icon. Do not be surprised that you can drive your car or ride a bus to within 100 yards of this exquisite scene—the most often visited place near Aspen outside of downtown. Whether you visit here once or a thousand times, you will experience the ultimate in tranquility at this centerpiece of nature.

The Formation of Peaks and Streams and Valleys and Lakes

It is difficult to comprehend that close to 300 million years ago the origins of the Maroon Formation developed through extensive deposits of sand and mud by massive floodwaters into a Pennsylvanian to Permian seaway. Believe it or not, during this time, Colorado was located near the equator. Eventually the flat layers of sedimentary

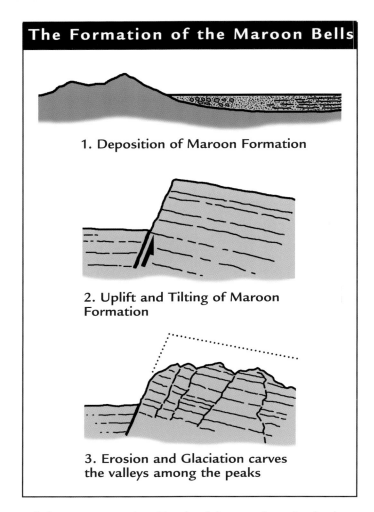

The Formation of the Maroon Bells

1. Deposition of Maroon Formation

2. Uplift and Tilting of Maroon Formation

3. Erosion and Glaciation carves the valleys among the peaks

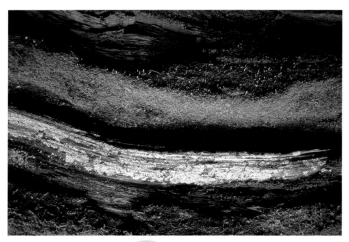

38 **Moss on log–Buckskin Pass**

deposits, with depths over 2 miles thick, solidified into the iron-rich Maroon Formation. During the Laramide Orogeny some 70 to 65 million years ago, tremendous blocks of land mass along faultlines were lifted up and tilted leading to the formation

of the present-day Rocky Mountains, including the Maroon Bells, Pyramid Peak and Sievers Mountain. In recent geologic times, between 2 million and 15,000 years ago, the Earth experienced periodic cooling episodes with persistent accumulations of snow forming huge glaciers up to 3,000 feet thick. As the glaciers advanced and retreated, they methodically carved the deep U-shaped valleys we see today. Through catastrophic rock falls and avalanches, debris clogged the valleys, forming lakes. All this action compressed through millions of years has created this exquisite system of mountains and valleys.

A Wilderness Walk in the Back and Beyond

Beyond the doorstep of Maroon Lake lies the Maroon Bells-Snowmass Wilderness. On a walk through the heart of this wilderness, you will find much more than what led you to its entrance. Colorado's fourth-largest wilderness area has 181,000 acres, six peaks

over 14,000 feet and more than 100 miles of trails. One of the most popular loops links more than 28 miles of trails over four rugged alpine mountain passes above 12,000 feet circumnavigating the Maroon Bells. The walk at a leisurely pace can take upward of seven days, comfortably within five days. Regardless of whether you backpack or rent a llama to carry your gear, you'll find the route over West Maroon Pass (12,500 feet), Frigid Air Pass (12,415 feet), Trail Rider Pass (12,420 feet) and Buckskin Pass (12,500 feet) features vistas of picturesque valleys and basins. The terrain extends through three major life zones: the montane, subalpine and alpine. A variety of plant and animal communities depend on the direction and degree of slope, drainage and moisture available, exposure to wind, soil type, fire history and other significant microbiological and environmental factors. Rest assured, you will not be disappointed by its unspoiled beauty especially from mid-July through early August. Mountain slopes and valley meadows are filled with a plethora of colorful wildflowers, green tree-lined wetlands, and exquisite non-woody life in the form of sedges, rushes, mosses, lichen and

liverwort. As lush as this environment appears during the midst of summer, it is a harsh environment the rest of the year. In winter temperatures drop well below freezing, hurricane-type winds scour the land of winter snows and vegetation, spring thaws gorge streams with the power of eroding snowmelt and summer thunderstorms pelt the cirques with torrential rains. Despite the harshness of this environment, many creatures have adapted to these climate variances. As you walk, keep an eye out for all kinds of animals, from elk, mule deer, bighorn sheep, yellowbelly marmot, pika and beaver to porcupine, meadow vole, spruce squirrel, shrew, coyote, red fox and weasel.

A walk through Maroon Bells-Snowmass Wilderness is more than an outdoor experience for nature lovers. It might be an epic personal journey for those who do not frequent the back of beyond for solace, or a rare photographic opportunity for the adventurous photographer.

Photographing Maroon Bells-Snowmass Wilderness

An initial visit to Maroon Bells-Snowmass Wilderness may be a call to come back again and again or a one-time photographic opportunity to photograph the ever-enticing reflection of Maroon Bells on Maroon Lake. No matter how many times you visit, weather, time of day and season of the year will affect how and what you photograph. If you plan to walk to the edge of the lake no more than a hundred yards from the trailhead, you are assured of a great shot by being there at the first light of day. If you're looking to explore and photograph all ends of the wilderness, you will need to prepare your gear much differently. Trails into the Maroon Bells-Snowmass Wilderness can be accessed at road's end via Maroon Lake, West Maroon Creek, Capitol Creek from the Aspen side of the area or the old mining town of Ashcroft to Conundrum Creek and Cathedral Peak. Beyond these portals is an extensive network of hiking trails traversing and circumnavigating the wilderness. Be well prepared if you are going on a multiday excursion into the backcountry with or without camera equipment. Outlined below are some helpful guidelines to prepare for a backpacking trip or for a day's walk from your car.

Maroon Lake

There are two ways of getting to Maroon Lake: either by riding the bus from the base of

40 **Wildflower at Maroon Lake meadow**

Aspen Highlands during peak daytime hours or by car first thing in the morning or late in the evening after the buses have stopped operating. If you arrive earlier than 8 a.m. or after 6 p.m. during the spring, summer and fall months when the Maroon Creek Road is open, take Maroon Creek Road off Highway 82 heading from the roundabout at their juncture and drive about 9.5 miles on this narrow, paved two-lane road to Maroon Lake parking lot. There are extensive paved lots and plenty of spaces as long as you arrive early.

There are a number of turnouts, campgrounds and trailheads to stop at along the way up the road for photographs. Maroon Creek flows through this deep V-shaped valley lined with aspen trees and dramatic red rock formations running up mountain cirques. The vistas are otherworldly. In an exceptionally wet year a wide range of wildflowers explodes into the brightest colors. During the fall sometime between the last week of September and the first few days of October, the aspen turn gold, lighting up the mountains. Look up to find Pyramid Peak dominating the skyline in the distance. Then as you near the last one and a half miles to Maroon Lake, the Maroon Bells pull you toward the road's end.

Photographing a reflection on Maroon Lake is best at sunrise just as the first sunlight sweeps the upper reaches of the jagged Maroon Peaks. Set up your tripod anywhere on the north edge of the lake's shoreline. One word of caution: you will not be the only one photographing this morning so be courteous and understanding of other photographers' desires to fill their viewfinders with a pristine perspective without other people in the shot. Arrive early to select your preferred location up to a half hour before sunrise. A wide angle lens starting at 20 to 24mm and ranging up to about 50mm allows you to capture the unique symmetry of the peaks and the valley. Work the setting in both vertical and horizontal formats. The unique features of setting up close to the drainage on the east end of the lake are the layers of rock in the bottom of the lake that replicate those found in the striation on the Maroon Peaks through the lake's reflection near the shore out to about 50 feet. You may be treated to some great lighting theatrics especially if there are broken clouds streaming over the peaks or

41 Winter reflection on Maroon Lake

billowy cumulus clearing from their craggy horizon line. You may even try stepping away from the lake to frame the peaks between a window in the aspens on the northeast end of the meadow. Or compose a shot with wildflowers in full bloom in the foreground to add color and scale to the image. Step back from the shoreline to make a photograph with all the photographers there with you to photograph this awe-inspiring vista. If you want a great winter shot, stop in at the T-Lazy 7 Ranch and arrange a guided snowmobile ride to the lake. Try early December when the lake is not fully frozen, and depart from the ranch a half hour before sunrise. Bring snowshoes or cross-country skis to amble about the lake to get your best perspectives. Try timing your excursion as a winter storm is approaching with sunlight on the peaks. Once you have taken your reflection photograph, don't stop. Hone a longer lens 180 to 200mm on the southeast shoreline nearest the drainage where foliage hangs on a small cliff disappearing into the lake. The great sloping and diverging lines of rock along the edge of the shore create an interesting mosaic and reflection on the lake. If the light is good on the Maroon Bells, look due north by northeast to

Ptarmigan

42) On the trail Buckskin Pass to Snowmass Peak—Maroon Bells-Snowmass Wilderness

the slopes leading up to Sievers Peak. The first light fills ridgelines full of aspen, offset by shadows running divergent lines through the valleys against the crag lines of the peaks. As the morning progresses with light filling the valley, walk the trail west along the shore. The meadow is filled with a range of wildflowers, and you may even find a new perspective with peaks reflecting on the lake's surface. In the fall, if you can time your visit to arrive at the edge of the lake as the first snowstorm is clearing from the peaks and the golden leaves of the trees quake, you will be rewarded with one of the most beautiful landscapes in Colorado. Oftentimes broken clouds soften the scene and dispersed shafts of light dance across the peaks and trees, creating a heavenly setting.

Within a Day's Walk: Snowmass Creek, Conundrum Creek and Cathedral Lake

There are a number of wonderful trails into the wilderness where day hikes lead to beautiful landscapes. Drive from Snowmass Village west on Bush Creek Road to Trail 1975 that meanders for 3 miles on rolling terrain along Snowmass Creek. You walk through massive groves of aspen for about a mile and a half before the trail opens into the deep V-shaped valley that Snowmass Creek runs through. The walk is worth the trouble, as it provides the opportunity to explore the plentiful detail of the aspen groves, and the river with high mountain peaks for great morning or evening photography. Travel south of Aspen on Forest

Service Road 102, known as Castle Creek Road, toward Ashcroft to the Conundrum Creek Trail 1981 exactly 5 miles from Highway 82, then right on Forest Road 128 1.1 miles to the trailhead. An 8.5-mile hike leads you to Conundrum Hot Springs. On your hike to Conundrum Valley, you'll find high sloping sides with fields of wildflowers, avalanche runs and beaver ponds farther up the trail toward the springs. This is a popular destination. The Cathedral Peak and Lake trailhead can be found 1 mile beyond the old mining town of Ashcroft by turning right, then driving .6 miles on an unpaved road to Trail 1984. This walk is best made in the morning. It is steep with sweeping grassy slopes filled with wildflowers and vistas with big mountain peaks. The reflection of Cathedral Peak at the lake is well worth the effort. Be prepared for thunderstorms if you plan to stay through the day into the evening. On day hikes, it is important to carry the essentials to sustain your energy and to protect yourself, plus just enough camera equip-

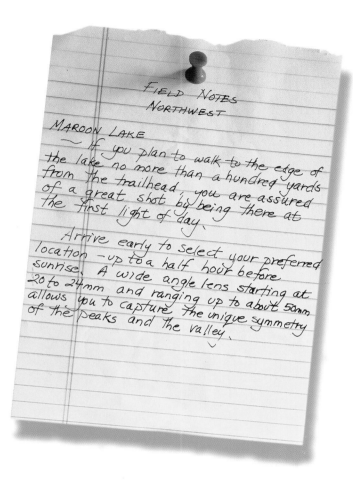

FIELD NOTES
NORTHWEST

MAROON LAKE
~ If you plan to walk to the edge of the lake no more than a hundred yards from the trailhead, you are assured of a great shot by being there at the first light of day.

Arrive early to select your preferred location – up to a half hour before sunrise. A wide angle lens starting at 20 to 24mm and ranging up to about 50mm allows you to capture the unique symmetry of the peaks and the valley.

43 **Sievers Mountain**

ment to get the shots you are after. Set your limits to a maximum of three lenses, a body and tripod. Galen Rowell, the late landscape photographer, suggested carrying a bean bag

instead of a tripod to reduce your load. It is easy enough to balance the bean bag on natural objects or your backpack instead of using a tripod. Go as light as possible. Gear should not deter you from having a memorable photographic experience.

Out on the Trail– Risk Taking and Words of Caution

A backcountry excursion into the wilderness is filled with thousands of photographic opportunities, some riskier than others. Risk taking can greatly enhance your opportunity to capture an amazing photograph rarely made. Walking in high places includes exposure to sudden shifts in fast-moving, localized weather systems that can rout your adventure or increase the potential for that unexpected moment. Often the most beautiful photographs are made on the leading edge, in the midst or tail end of a summer thunderstorm. Broken clouds with shafts of warm evening light streaming down on a glistening land-

44 **North shoreline reflection on Maroon Lake**

scape are the extraordinary moments photographers dream about. Yet caution must be exercised or your outing may turn into a

catastrophic misadventure. Minimize your exposure on high ridges or mountain slopes in mid-afternoon where lightning may strike. Know your limits and ability to move quickly. Carry a lightweight tent or tarp to create shelter during the midst of a torrential shower with high winds. Most of all, make sure your camera gear is dry and easily accessible when that moment does occur—you will need to move very quickly.

45 **Willow Lake in Maroon Bells-Snowmass Wilderness**

46 Entrance to Starvation Valley on the Yampa River

Dinosaur National Monument

The Tale of Two Rivers, Dinosaurs and the Douglass Quarry

This is a story about a remarkable place like no other in the West. This is classic desert canyon country, complemented by rugged mountainous areas. This tale of two rivers begins in Colorado and ends at the Douglass Quarry in Utah. Before the Yampa River flowed into the Green, splitting a

47 Douglass Quarry in Dinosaur National Monument

mountain ridgetop in two for 7 miles, there were dinosaurs. Before the ancient Fremont people made their home here and carved petroglyphs on the sandstone walls near Echo Park thousands of years ago, there were dinosaurs. Before fur trader William H. Ashley floated down the Green in 1825, and before legendary explorer/scientist John Wesley Powell led his famous 1869 expedition down the Green River and out

41

through the Grand Canyon, there were dinosaurs. Before Patrick Lynch homesteaded in Echo Park in 1883, there were dinosaurs. Before Earl Douglass, a paleontologist from the Carnegie Museum in Pittsburgh scoured this land in 1908 and 1909 searching for dinosaur bones, there were dinosaurs. Before the site where the Douglass Quarry sits today was designated a national monument in 1915, and before the canyons of the Green and Yampa Rivers were added to the original park in 1938, there were dinosaurs. Before Sierra Club President David Brower lobbied Congress to stop the building of the dam below Echo Park in 1955 that would have flooded and buried the Green and Yampa Rivers forever, and long before the memory of human beings, dinosaurs roamed this land as

48) **Desert Paintbrush**

far back as 150 million years ago.

An ancient river meandered through this area during the Jurassic Period. Paleological evidence supports the idea that dinosaur bones became embedded in the sandy bottom of the river or were washed up on an ancient river bend's sandbar during a great spring flood. It remains unknown why and the list of questions as to how is long, yet we

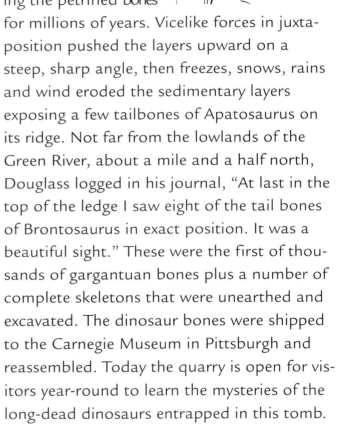

Canyon Wren

know that dinosaurs became extinct some 65 million years ago. Through the ages layers and layers of sand and mud piled one on top of another as rivers and seas existed, then dried, preserving the petrified bones for millions of years. Vicelike forces in juxtaposition pushed the layers upward on a steep, sharp angle, then freezes, snows, rains and wind eroded the sedimentary layers exposing a few tailbones of Apatosaurus on its ridge. Not far from the lowlands of the Green River, about a mile and a half north, Douglass logged in his journal, "At last in the top of the ledge I saw eight of the tail bones of Brontosaurus in exact position. It was a beautiful sight." These were the first of thousands of gargantuan bones plus a number of complete skeletons that were unearthed and excavated. The dinosaur bones were shipped to the Carnegie Museum in Pittsburgh and reassembled. Today the quarry is open for visitors year-round to learn the mysteries of the long-dead dinosaurs entrapped in this tomb.

The Great Canyons of Dinosaur

The Green River flows into the canyon from the northeast by southwest from the grassy park land below Browns Park through the Gates of Lodore. The entrance to Lodore Canyon was named by one of John Wesley

49 Old tree reflection at Deerlodge Park—Yampa River

Canyon was named by one of John Wesley Powell's men from a poem describing a waterfall in the Lake District of northwest England, referring to the canyon waters as "recoiling, turmoiling, and toiling, and boiling." The prominent rock formation of the steep, narrow canyon stair-stepped walls is Precambrian Uinta Mountain Quartzite.

Farther south by east the Yampa River enters the canyon near Deerlodge Park, a grassy shoreline meadow with a canopy of huge cottonwoods. Deerlodge Park is an oasis before the river-carved canyon walls of Weber Sandstone and

50 Cottonwoods at Deerlodge Park

Morgan Formations. The Green and Yampa join at Echo Park where the river meanders around Steamboat Rock. This massive slick-rock feature dominates the valley vista and is surrounded by sheer symmetrical cliffs of Pennsylvanian/Permian Weber Sandstone. About 2 miles downstream at Mitten Park, a major fault forms a sweeping jagged-edge ridgeline that dips from the heights of the canyon walls through the Green River channel, then swoops dramatically up the other side. This feature is known as the Mitten Park Fault. Down river through Whirl Pool

Canyon, deep red vertical walls feature Uinta Mountain Group sandstone that disappears within 3 miles after leaving Mitten Park. The Green washes out and meanders through Island-Rainbow Park where the Morrison Formation provides an apparent rainbow of colors, and sandstone bluffs and rolling mounds dominate the landscape. Aside from the highly publicized dinosaur finds at the quarry, throughout the park, marine invertebrate fossils are more numerous than their popular dinosaur counterparts, confirming the presence of inland seas that dominated the land eons ago.

On the west edge of Island Park the river enters the magnificent stair-stepped canyon doors of Split Mountain where steep cliff faces of limestone and sandstone outcroppings dominate the rugged strata of siltstone and shale. Here the river has carved down the center of the mountain dividing it in two, thus the name Split Mountain. Powell was astonished by this phenomena at

51 Anderson Hole on the Yampa River

first sight, and upon closer exploration after climbing to the top of the anticline, confirmed his observation that the river had actually cut through the top of the mountain ridgeline for more than 8 miles. The exit of Split Mountain is marked by deep curves carved through Weber Sandstone that slope into sagebrush-filled rolling hills and river bottom plains.

Along these rivers there are diverse ecosystems and habitat for an equally diverse range of wildlife. The rugged mountains are a patchwork of juniper, piñon, ponderosa pine, and Douglas fir mixed with aspen. Elk, moose, mule deer, mountain lion and bobcat roam the high range with coyotes, badgers and skunks making their home in the rocky parts of this area. Bench and plateau lands above the river basins are dominated by piñon pines and juniper with a mix of sage and big sagebrush hugging the ground. Along the steep canyon slopes and sheer

52 Yampa River at Harding Hole

44

53 **Harding Hole overlook–the Yampa River**

rock walls are drought-resistant conifers. Saltbush, greasewood, mountain mahogany, serviceberry, rabbitbrush, Mormon Tea, currant and prickly pear compete for any remnant of highly alkaline soils. Bighorn sheep can be seen scampering with their young on these walls above the rivers, as can a plethora of birds, including bald eagles, wrens, hawks, owls, turkey vultures, ravens, swallows, warblers, flycatchers and jays. The constant call of the canyon wren echoing through the cliffs is a reminder that this is an amazing place.

Until recently, shorebank riparian zones on both tributaries were scoured by spring floods and only the hardiest varieties of grasses, willows and trees could survive. Since Flaming Gorge Dam was built, plant life has changed dramatically along the banks of the

Green above the confluence of the Yampa. There has been a marked decline in cottonwood, box elder, yellow and sandbar willow, which have been supplanted by the non-native tamarisk. Creatures with prehistoric ancestral roots inhabiting the waterways are these fish: Colorado pikeminnow, razorback sucker, bonytail and humpback chub. They are nearing extinction as they depend on high spring flows and summer warm water temperatures for their success. The Green and Yampa River region is one of the few places in Colorado where North America's largest insect, the Dobson fly, makes its home, creating a reliable food source for fish. Utah tiger salamanders, leopard frogs, Rocky Mountain toads, garter snakes and Great Basin gopher snake are reptile and amphibian species occasional to this habitat. Beaver and otter are less common than might be anticipated, yet find the banks of the rivers excellent habitat to thrive. These waterways are home to significant population of geese, blue heron, sandpiper, ducks, gulls and grebes. In spite of the human threat of encroachment to these wild lands and creatures, Dinosaur National Monument remains a pristine sanctuary for all who call it home and those who visit.

Photographing Dinosaur National Monument

Dinosaur is an immense desert wilderness. Photographing it can be a logistical challenge and one of the ultimate backcountry experiences. Monument and Bureau of Land Management roads lead to its edge, where you will find expansive vistas with the river winding into the distance. There are a number of locations to visit that can yield exceptional results.

Echo Park–Take the monument's entrance off Highway 40 just 2 miles east of the town of Dinosaur and wind your way about 34 miles to Echo Park. Steamboat Rock can be easily photographed at sunrise or sunset. During these calmer hours its reflection across the surface of the Green can provide an excellent perspective indicative of the geology found in the monument. Explore the nearby walls for ancient petroglyphs, or walk back up the road about 1.25 miles from the valley campground to Whispering Cave.

Browns Park and the Gates of Lodore
Just west of the town of Maybell take Highway 318 north to either Browns Park Wildlife Refuge for a variety and abundance of wildlife, or find fly fisherman working the gold medal trout water below Flaming Gorge Reservoir. If you are looking for a remarkable landscape image, a view of the entry to the Canyon of Lodore, known as the Gates of Lodore, follow the signs to County Road 24 to the river runners putin and ranger station—it's best to work this location in the morning from pre-dawn through sunrise. Work the southeast bank of the river along the shoreline and hike up the hillside above the meadow on the same side of the river for a wider perspective. In the spring wildflowers are in abundance, especially Indian paintbrush and prickly pear cactus. Photographing is best done from the shoreline of either river, on side canyon hikes or at the edge of the canyon's rim.

Douglass Quarry–The Douglass Quarry is the monument's center stage for information

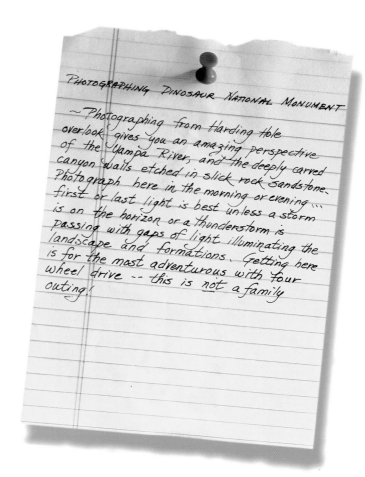

PHOTOGRAPHING DINOSAUR NATIONAL MONUMENT

~ Photographing from Harding Hole overlook gives you an amazing perspective of the Yampa River, and the deeply carved canyon walls etched in slick rock sandstone. Photograph here in the morning or evening... first or last light is best unless a storm is on the horizon or a thunderstorm is passing with gaps of light illuminating the landscape and formations. Getting here is for the most adventurous with four wheel drive -- this is _not_ a family outing!

about the Park. It boasts a cleverly designed theme-park ride back in time, as if you were entering Jurassic Park. A visit to the Douglass Quarry is imperative if you wish to understand Dinosaur National Monument and the archeological finds made by Douglass. The well-preserved, exposed dinosaur bones are the main thrust of any photograph made here. Yet it might well be how visitors interact with and react to the power of this massive effort in excavation that can drive the subject matter of photographs here. Of equal interest is the area where staff worked for several years to delicately extricate bones, cleaning them and then cataloging them.

The main area of the quarry has extremely good available light to photograph the dinosaur bones, not to mention the heavy equipment and rail system used to extract and move bones weighing tons of pounds. A zoom lens will help isolate significant clusters and artifacts on the main wall where the bones are exposed. If the light is subdued from the outside, fill flash may be necessary to accentuate people investigating the dig for the first time. Working the quarry is a great place to photograph a cultural exhibit as if you were on a documentary assignment for a monthly publication. And there are as many photographic pieces to this story as there are exposed dinosaur bones of this ancient riverbed.

Collard Lizard

Harding Hole Overlook Adventure—A side trip away from the madding crowds and the main roads of the monument could lead you to places like Mantle Ranch and Wagon Wheel Gap. This excursion is recommended for adventurous, backroads four-wheel-vehicle drivers only.

Directions to Harding Hole—From Elk Springs on Highway 40 take Bear Valley Road (County Road 14) 16 miles west and stay right at the fork on Yampa Bench Road (County Road 14). Follow Yampa Bench Road (an unimproved winding, dusty, red dirt road) for approximately 9 to 10 miles and park to the side of the road and follow the trail out to the edge of the overlook.

Photographing from the overlook gives you an amazing perspective of the Yampa River, and the deeply carved canyon walls etched in slickrock sandstone. Photograph here in the morning or evening—first or last light is best unless a storm is on the horizon or a thunderstorm is passing with gaps of light illuminating the landscape and formations. If you are interested, walk back out to the dirt road and head east about half a mile to the Bull Canyon trail and walk down to the river. Photographing from the river channel up can lend power to your composition with the water rushing by. Watch for detail in the form of texture and the juxtaposition of the varying landscape and formations. This is a steep, intermediate to difficult hike, and will take about an hour to an hour and a half going down. The hike from the river up through Bull Canyon is strenuous and may take a couple of hours or more. Plan for weather and for darkness, if you go in the late afternoon.

Colorado National Monument

54 **The Pipe Organ at Colorado National Monument**

Legend of John Otto

Among Colorado's gems in the hallowed halls of beauty, Colorado National Monument shines with the brightest. Grand views and an incomparable set of natural wonders are a short drive from the Grand Valley and the city of Grand Junction. Within the monument, the landscape is dominated by towering ancient desert sandstone monoliths, and groups of spires are enveloped in canyon walls by a one-way downward sloping monocline or "one-sided fold and uplift" north toward the Colorado River Basin and the Book Cliffs farther on. As you drive the switchbacks climbing into the monument, you might envision the monument as a distant imaginary land on another planet. Actually, the monument sits at the easternmost edge of the vast Colorado

55 **Lone pine at Rattlesnake Arches**

Plateau that extends through Utah's Arches and Canyonlands National Parks, Bryce and Zion Canyons, to Arizona's Grand Canyon and the northwestern edge of Colorado's Umcompahgre Plateau. Subtleties and diversity in plant ecosystems and range in wildlife are amazingly comparable to those in Dinosaur National Monument. Relative to human history and certainly within a fleeting moment in Earth's geologic development, it took the famous United States Geologic Survey photographer William Henry Jackson on assignment with the Denver and Rio Grande Railroad in 1882 and Grand Junction boosters to initiate the fight for the monument's national registry. Yet, one man's efforts stand out above all others completing the necessary charge to bring Colorado National Monument to life—the legendary John Otto.

John Otto was a reclusive man by all accounts of his last 20 years before he died of a heart attack near his boyhood home of Yreka, California in 1952. He came to Grand Junction in the early part of the 20th century and fell in love with the area that became the Colorado National Monument. He lived alone in the wild canyon country he traversed by burro, setting down the first road at the east end of the monument that visitors walk today on Serpents Trail. Contrary to his character of later years, he was considered a

56 The Pipe Organ in a dust storm

"flamboyant, get-things-done kind of guy" throughout the Grand Valley in his earlier years.

So strong was his passion for this place that he single-hand-edly convinced the Grand Junction Chamber of Commerce and citizenry to join him in an extensive letter-writing campaign to Interior Secretary James A. Garfield beginning in 1907. On May 24, 1911, President William Howard Taft declared the 23,000-acre park a national monument. According to Michael O'Boyle, in the article "John Otto Honored Fifty Years After His Death," "He was a man who cared little for his own prosperity, a man who lived his life for the betterment of his community and his country." His compensation as custodian of the monument was a symbolic $1 per month. The magnitude that all the Colorado National Monument embodies is a tribute to John Otto, the first custodian of the park from 1911 to 1927.

Independence Monument– Sculpting a Geologic Icon

Although there are a significant number of geologic features and formations of equal importance in the monument, Independence Monument is the one icon that exemplifies this place. Towering among oddly shaped mesas, this spire rises 500 feet above the valley floor at the head of two canyons, sitting below the rim of the upper plateau. Except for the rock layers exposed at the deeper reaches of the canyon floor whose origins date back some 1.7 billion years, most of the mesas and monoliths found here are the results of the rising and receding of seas, deposits of sediment, uplift of land masses and erosion by wind, rain, rivers and ice during the Mesozoic Era some 225 to 65 million years ago. Most of the structural framework of the monument occurred during the Laramide Orogeny that began in the Late Cretaceous time, about 70 million years ago, and continuing into the middle of the Eocene period about 50 million years ago. These are extensive acts of tremendous geologic forces moving slowly and powerfully. Observe how these actions have shaped free-standing Independence Monument. According to renowned geologist Jack Rathbone, "You can see a thin cap of resistant sandstone belong-

57 Last light at Independence Monument at Colorado National Monument

ing to the Triasic Kayenta Formation protecting the underlying softer Wingate Sandstone from erosion. The slope-forming section at the base of the tower consists of shales and siltstones belonging to the Triasic Chinle Formation. The Kodel Canyon fault lies to the north behind the Monument. Notice how the sandstones in the left distance dip suddenly and steeply to the northeast, as they become sheared and broken along the faultline." On a less scientific note, John Otto originally named the tower the Jefferson Monument, and first climbed it on Flag Day, placing the Stars and Stripes on top in 1911. Until he left, Otto climbed Jefferson Monument each July 4th, raising the American flag in celebration of our nation's independence. In later years, the name of the spire changed and was noted on park maps by 1950.

Independence Monument

Kayenta Formation

Wingate Sandstone

Chinle Formation

Talus and Rubble

58 **Coke Ovens in snow at Colorado National Monument**

Photographing Colorado National Monument

Pull out the map, go to the visitors center and get to know the Monument before you dive headlong into making photographs literally sight unseen. Learn about the plant and wildlife, read about the geology of the land and key features, the surrounding topography and terrain nearby and far away, and make notes or at least mental notes about the features that most interest you. Look at images in books, on post cards and made into posters of the Monument. Get an idea of the time of day and the general locations where these photographers made the image. Ask a park ranger to pinpoint on the map how to get there, they will be more than glad to volunteer information on just about everything. Consider your options: whether to drive to the most highly visited attractions or whether to take some time for a short hike that might lend a different perspective than that of the throngs of visitors a step ahead of you. The monument is usually quiet in the spring and fall.

Pipe Organ–Go directly to Book Cliffs View Point area less than a half mile from the visitors center and head to the Canyon Rim Trail for a short walk three-quarters of a mile along the rim's edge. Walk around a bit to get to know the location and what might be the most interesting perspective depending on the time of day you arrive. The most notable view of the Pipe Organ is looking southeast from the rim's edge or just slightly pulled back. Photograph at first light in the morning or late evening at this location. Try different focal length lenses to attain perspective of the formation. Set up with a wide angle lens 20 to 28mm with a piñon pine or the broken Triasic Kayenta cap in the foreground with the formation off in the distance to create interest. Concentrate on making sure the foreground, middle and background are in sharp focus. Consider using a small aperture setting F22 or 32, and slower shutter speed to increase depth of field and color saturation during the exposure. Try using a longer length lens between 105 to 200mm to bring your perspective in tight on the three spires and their bulging bases as light dances across the sandstone strata to highlight their intricate detail. Consider using a larger F2.8 to mid range F8 to 11 aperture setting and faster shutter speed to soften the background and foreground with the spires in sharp focus to define the subject you desire the viewer to see.

Mountain Lion

Independence Monument—The traditional perspectives of Independence Monument are from Otto's trail or from its designated overlook at the turnout. Easy enough to find and get to. From this approach this is definitely a late afternoon or evening shot, most desirably with some dramatic light or atmospheric conditions. Yet to really get a feel of the Monument it is well worth making a predawn hike up Monument Canyon Trail past the spire by a half mile for a sunrise shoot. This is a lengthy and aggressive 3- to 4-mile walk up a medium to steep grade so give yourself about 2 hours lead time at least. Don't forget your flashlight unless hiking during a full moon. Upon arrival you will find you are in the shadows of the canyon wall running south to north set to your northeast. This is a great place to be just after a spring rain or first fall snow. Set up on a small elevated ridge (be careful to stay on the trail or scramble on rocks to leave no trace of your visit), to make it appear that the viewer sees the foreground as if you were suspended in space. Plan your visit when a full moon is setting to the west over the spire at sunrise. Even better yet, catch it with partly cloudy skies filled with billowing cumulus. No doubt this will add perspective and drama to your photograph.

Sweeping Vistas of the Grand Valley and Book Cliffs—The views looking northeast from any of the overlooks through Red, Ute or Wedding Canyons are spectacular. However, you might find the perspective from the Highland viewpoint advantageous as well. If you are interested in eliminating any remnants of the build out in the Grand Valley with the Book Cliffs in the background, you are really going to have to work to find just the right spot before composing your photograph. Yet it might be just as well to capture the downward sloping perspective of the monocline with the lights of the city lit just before dawn or at last light with warm fill light bouncing off high clouds gracing the valley before you during a tremendous sunset. These exposures are often made with the largest aperture value and slowest shutter speeds possible—F22 or 32. Rim Rock Drive viewpoints and designated turnouts plus a scramble up a hillside or down one of the trails leading to the canyon are exceptional places to capture these photographs.

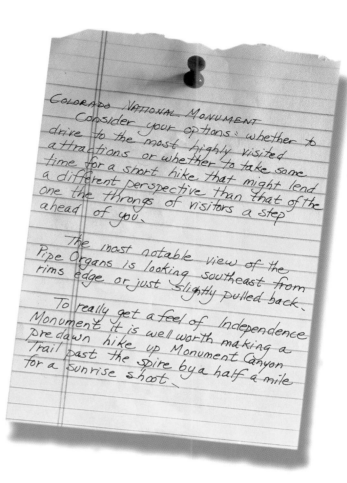

COLORADO NATIONAL MONUMENT
Consider your options: whether to drive to the most highly visited attractions or whether to take some time for a short hike that might lend a different perspective than that of the one the throngs of visitors a step ahead of you.

The most notable view of the Pipe Organs is looking southeast from rims edge or just slightly pulled back.

To really get a feel of Independence Monument it is well worth making a pre dawn hike up Monument Canyon Trail past the spire by a half a mile for a sunrise shoot.

59 **Old Stage Road in fall on Grand Mesa**

The Grand Mesa

It's easy to imagine why the Ute may have called the Grand Mesa "Thunder Mountain." You need only stand at the Lands End Overlook on the west edge of the mesa on an early summer afternoon, and watch lightning strikes and listen to the clap of thunder echo from Colorado National Monument to the Book Cliffs as a storm sweeps across the Grand Valley. During World War II while men were fighting overseas, legendary cowgirls like Winifred Raber herded and tended cattle during the summers in the lush green meadows high on the mesa. Likewise women and children escaped the summer heat of Delta and Grand Junction camping near lakes and streams while the men visited on weekends. It was no different for ancient "Archaic Cultures" whose stone spearheads and remnant campsites have been found on the mesa, indicating they also camped during summers to hunt deer and elk, and gather wild plants and berries.

The history and the stories told combine to fashion the folklore of the region. Yet there are some facts that cannot be disputed. Geologists are certain that, hidden beneath "the largest flat top mountain in the world," geologic secrets of how Thunder Mountain came to exist with a cap of volcanic basalt 200 to 600 feet thick are etched in the stone. Reddish and greenish glasslike silicate stones similar to quartz can be found on the mesa, indicating that the molten flows were from deep in the mantle of the earth. Look for some unique features known as Fens, made from ancient sedge peat from wetlands near Kannah Creek. The lakes here today are the last bits of work done by ice flows between 10,000 and 20,000 years ago. You might be surprised to learn that this is Colorado's "Land of Lakes"—up to 600 lakes and reservoirs are found on the top of the mesa. The Grand Mesa is one place you shouldn't pass by for more popular locations farther down the beaten path.

Photographing the Grand Mesa

The route is known as the Grand Mesa Scenic Byway between Interstate 70 on Highway 65 south over the monument down to the town of Cedaredge. There is a spur on top of the mesa that runs about 9 miles to Lands End Overlook. The scenic byway offers many vantage points on either the north or south side of the mesa. Either side offers excellent opportunities to photograph massive stands of quaking aspen in the fall or winter. The Mesa Lake area offers short hikes to nearby lakes, perfect places to find shapes and forms of trees and mosaics of colors reflecting on the lakes. As you near the top of the mesa from the north, there is an old dirt wagon road, on which you may find a wonderful spot to photograph, especially during the fall. Aspen literally form a canopy over the narrow road to create some interesting light plays as the road rolls away from you down a concaved sloping gradient.

It is best to catch the turn of the aspen on partly cloudy days or days when a storm is clearing with light splashing across tops of these huge stands. You may also find an opening on a rock outcropping that affords you a vista looking northwest across the tree-tops with the Book Cliffs off in the distance. This is a great evening shot at sunset. Take the spur off Highway 65 to Lands End Overlook for a great vista of the Grand Valley; this is a good place for an evening shot as a summer thunderstorm clears the valley. On the south side of the mesa near the top of the crest is a small U-shaped basin on the right or east side of the road. If you come in winter at mid to late morning, look for soft broken storm light to create an unusual divergence of vertical and horizontal shadow lines that appear in juxtaposition with trunks of the trees as they emerge from the snow.

The Grand Mesa is a special place to find a range of beautiful landscapes to photograph: extensive aspen stands, broad vistas, and serene lakes.

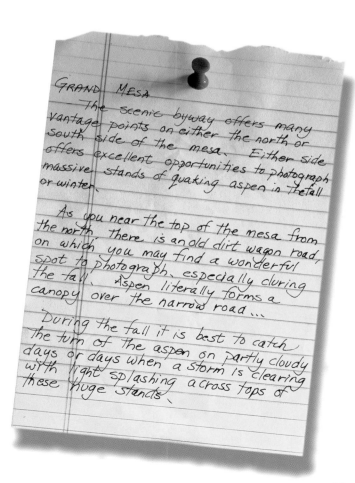

Dallas Divide

THE Southwest REGION

There are places found exclusively in Colorado's Southwest Region whose names are road signs through the lore of Western history. Today, these Old West outposts are must-see markers on the road map through scenic byways; the echo of history resonates in the names of the peaks of the rugged San Juan Mountains: Durango, Cimarron, Telluride, Ouray, Lake City, Crested Butte, Silverton, Pagosa Springs, Mesa Verde, and the Black Canyon of the Gunnison. Everything about this part of Colorado is on a scale all its own—big and vast. The roads wind up and

61 The road to Rico

over high-mountain passes leading to incomparable panoramic vistas—one after another. The peaks are compared to the Swiss

Alps near Ouray and for good reason. The old narrow gauge train from Durango to Silverton runs along the Animas River gorge where it stops for backpackers and climbers who make their way up to the Weminuche Wilderness via Chicago Basin to the heights of the Needles Mountains. The story about the Southwest is more than Western history and big peaks. It is

64 **Old barn near Durango**

a story about the Ancient Puebloans who thrived in the canyons of Mesa Verde and the sparse mesas of Hovenweep, leaving quietly and mysteriously for more hospitable climes to the south in New Mexico. Moreover, the Southwest of Colorado is about lifestyle and its tie to the Native Americans who still make it their home. All things wild living within its bound-

aries are suited to this place as much as it is to them. It stands to reason that the people who made this land their home yesterday and today possess a character equal to the landscape, strong and rugged. Nothing understated. Everything pronounced. It grabs your attention from a distance and draws you closer as if personally calling your name. In the

63 **Wilson Peak near Telluride**

challenge of the call to the Southwest, there is a genuine charm and warmth that is uniquely Colorado. This is a part of Colorado you do not want to miss.

65) **Square Tower House-Mesa Verde**

Mesa Verde National Park

Ancestral Links

The excavated cliff dwellings are the prominent features that will be of most interest to a first-time visitor. They are the draw enticing you to go on your own scientific mission. Here you'll find thousands of clues to a culture that thrived for hundreds of years, leaving as many questions as answers to be found in their dwellings. These architectural features are the cultural link to the Ancestral Puebloans who inhabited the alcoves in these cliffs for an estimated 700 years or more. The excavated dwellings you find here were built between A.D. 1190 and late 1280—the culmination of this people's advancement. This is Mesa Verde National Park, where nothing appears as simple as you first think. This is especially true about how this place came to be and how the cliff dwellers lived.

The Geologic Foundation

Sixteenth-century Spanish explorers gave Mesa Verde its adopted name—meaning "Green Table." The mesa itself is one of the largest in the region. The formations found in

66 Fog rolling into Mesa Verde

this geological group from top to bottom are Cliff House Sandstone, Menefee Formation and Point Lookout Sandstone, known as the Mesa Verde Formation. The Mesa Verde Group sits atop the oldest Mancos Shale Formation found in the bottom of the valleys throughout the Park. During the Cretaceous Period some 65 to 80 million years ago, seas flooded the area depositing sediment thousands of feet thick. As the waters crested and receded, different layers of sandstone developed. There was a massive uplifting of the area that accompanied the development of the nearby ancestral San Juan Mountains.

These mountains were worn flat through erosion over tens of millions of years and then another massive set of uplifts occurred. Finally, in recent times, geologically speaking, glaciers and streams eroded the San Juan Mountains, and created the valleys running through and around the Park. You can even find small stones and rocks from the San Juans left by these glaciers. Yet it is the slow erosive powers of wind and water combined with the process of freezing and thawing that put the finishing touches on the sandstone alcoves under which the Ancestral Puebloans made their homes.

The Ancestral Puebloans of Mesa Verde

The name Ancestral Puebloans has replaced the Navajo word for these people—*Anasazi*. Recently, Anasazi has been construed as

Rattlesnake

derogatory toward indigenous peoples, being translated as "the ancient enemy." After their total and hasty departure from the mesa around A.D.1280, these people probably moved southwest to where the contemporary Puebloans make their home in New Mexico and Arizona today. Thus the name Ancestral Puebloans has been adopted.

Beyond their name, these people left no written historical epitaph of their daily lives except for a significant number of artifacts. Their masonry, architecture, foot paths, irrigation reservoirs and ditches, scrapers, awls, drills, stone knives, clay pottery, remnants of garments, split willow woven baskets, turkey feather blankets, yucca sandals, trash and pictographs and petroglyphs are the clues they did leave. In and around these ancient structures, paleontologists and archeologists have worked to discover and catalogue the vast wealth of information leading to basic scientific suppositions about daily life around the mesa. They look to modern Pueblo people in New Mexico and Arizona to understand the nature of the clans and families at Mesa Verde. There is a good chance that several generations lived closely together in the same building complex such as Cliff Palace or Spruce Tree House. Masons used sandstone and mortar to build with and added rooms as needed. There are numerous styles of masonry that evolved within one generation or passed onto the next.

You can imagine the voices of children at play and elders chanting from the depths of their kiva during a daily ceremonial gathering. Kiva is the Hopi word for ceremonial room. Commonly found at the center of the villages, kivas are prominent semicircular or circular underground chambers with wood beams and mud-covered roofs.

Most of the cliff dwellers' time was spent growing crops and hunting for wild game. Their only domesticated animals were dogs and turkeys. During the summer months, life was made on the plaza in front of the dwellings; during the harsh winter months, it was lived inside their stone dwellings. Look to the Park's visitor's guides with artist renderings to gain a more realistic visual interpretation of daily life at Cliff Palace or of clans of people working in the fields tending crops on the mesa. The paintings are a way to extrapolate in simple terms how things might have been for these people. By comparison to contemporary American standards, life was not easy, and undoubtedly, it was short.

Mesa Verde National Park

The Ancestral Puebloans left a legacy that has been preserved by the founding of the Park. Close to 5,000 sites have been identified in the Park's boundary, and 600 of them are cliff dwellings. This is the largest archeological preserve in the country. The Park's story began long before Euro-Americans arrived to explore the mesa. Southern Ute knew of Mesa Verde before Spaniards named it. They kept far away from this sacred land, possibly in honor of the people who lived here long before they did. Some acted as guides to the Euro-Americans who would lay claim to fame for their original finds without mention of those who knew this place and led them to its treasures.

The evolution of Mesa Verde into a Park took some unusual twists and turns. A number of expeditions came close to Mesa Verde, but none reported any sign of dwellings from an ancient civilization. It wasn't known until 1874, when noted photographer William Henry Jackson, in charge of the Photographic Division of the U.S. Geological and Geographic Survey of the Territories made the first recorded visit to Mesa Verde. Apparently he received a tip from a prospector near Silverton named Tom Cooper who in turn had learned of the dwellings from a miner named Captain Ross. It is probable that the first non-native to have found the cliff dwellings was a prospector. Jackson made the first photographic record of the cliff dwellings.

Virginia Donaghe McClurg, a reporter from the *New York Graphic*, came to Colorado in 1886 to study the lost cities of Indians in the Southwest. She claims credit with the finds of Three Tiered House and Echo Cliff House. Her exploration of Balcony House may have motivated her in her preservation efforts. In 1888, the story goes, Richard Wetherill, along with his brother-in-law, Charles Mason of the noted Wetherill ranching family from Mancos, rode their horses in a winter storm onto the mesa looking for stray cattle where they discovered Cliff Palace, Spruce Tree House and Square Tower House. Richard

67 **Cliff Palace**

became impassioned, known for his skill for excavating the sites and cataloging the artifacts. Later he moved to Chaco Canyon, which is considered the nerve center of the Ancient Puebloan Nation, to excavate one of the most significant archeological finds in the West—Pueblo Bonito.

Next was Gustaf Nordenskiold from Sweden, who apparently came to Mancos to see the sights. He understood archeology well enough to have his camera shipped to the states and make 150 impeccable photographs, documenting the sites within the first three years of their discovery. He amassed a personal collection of 615 artifacts that he shipped to Sweden, and he wrote a book, *The Cliff Dwellers of the Mesa Verde,* published in 1893 upon his arrival home.

It was the sight of so many of the artifacts being taken that moved Virginia McClurg to wage one of the most aggressive campaigns ever to preserve a site as a national park. Writing poetry published in magazines, giving speeches and organizing more than 250,000 women across the country through the Federation of Women's Clubs, McClurg founded the Colorado Cliff Dwelling Association. The sole aim of the association was clear in its mission statement: "Restoration and preservation of the cliff and Pueblo ruins in the State of Colorado; the dissemination of knowledge concerning these prehistoric peoples; the collection of relics; and the acquiring of such property as is necessary to attain such objects."

Although she lobbied Congress for years, her efforts were rebuffed; however, she did negotiate a deal with Weminuche Ute Chief Ignacio to preserve the ruins, granting the Ute grazing rights in exchange for the land. Congress ratified the arrangement in 1901, giving the Colorado Cliff Dwelling Association control of the ruins. In frustration with Congress, McClurg went so far as to propose that Mesa Verde become a state park. This split the state and federal park effort into opposing factions, and it was finally quelled by Lucy Peabody, an influential women who lobbied Congress to adopt the bill making the area a national park in 1906.

The American people owe a great debt of gratitude to these two women who helped bring Mesa Verde National Park into existence with the signature of President Theodore Roosevelt. To keep looters from pilfering the sites of their treasures, the Antiquities Act was also passed in 1906, which prohibits looting on public lands. Mesa Verde has undergone extensive development and study since its inception and remains one of the true cultural

68 **Ladder in kiva entrance**

wonders of America's Native heritage.

Photographing Mesa Verde

This massive Park encompasses 52,122 acres, but do not be overwhelmed by its immensity. The Park entrance is located between Durango and Cortez near Mancos on Highway 160. Immediately upon entering the Park, you will be drawn to the cliff dwellings on Chapin Mesa or Wetherill Mesa at the southernmost reaches of the Park. Do not move hastily to these ends, as there is much to see and photograph between entering the Park and driving to these destinations. You will be treated to a spectacular drive up the North Rim to Morefield Village with expansive views of the La Plata Mountains directly across the valley and the San Juan Mountains to the northeast.

A sunset or sunrise shot at the Mancos Valley overlook is a great place to start. Over the past three years, significant fires have burned in the Park, creating unique opportunities to capture photos of the new growth of vegetation in late spring and early summer in contrast to the parched skeletons of piñons, junipers and burnt shrubs. Instead of avoiding the land denuded by fire, seek it out and pay close attention to detail while interpreting through your lens the changes that the fires have wrought upon the land, plants and wildlife of this arid climate. You may be surprised at what you find by moving slowly instead of hurriedly ahead. Vistas from the North Rim can be spectacular, especially in late spring where fog may stretch from the Montezuma Valley up the slopes of the mesa, creating some unusual lighting and dramatic atmospheric conditions to work from your well-researched location on the roadside. A stop at the Far View Visitors Center is a must to orient you in the park, and to purchase tickets to a guided tour. Once there, it will be helpful to see the published work of photographers in books and posters to learn where some of the most interesting perspectives can be had.

Photographing the cliff dwellings is predicated on where they are relative to sunrise from the east or sunset in the west and their position under the mesa rim. Taking a tour through the Cliff Palace late in the day or Balcony House in the morning can help you better understand their position relative to the rising and setting sun. You may find yourself working a location across the mesa focusing on a dwelling such as the Sunset House from Sun Point on the Mesa Top Loop Road. When the wind is blowing off the desert plains in the west, there can be dust in the air. The dust filters the direct sunlight making it appear softer and can increase it's warmth especially in the evening. When you are at the dwellings, observe the texture of the masonry, the layered design of the building structures, and the wood ladders leaning from the bottom of the kivas up to their entrances.

Try to avoid signage that may clutter your photographs and create a distraction. Walk these trails slowly, thoroughly examining every angle possible for locations you prefer to photograph them from. You have to work to find unique perches to eliminate unwanted shrubs from obstructing your photograph. Be mindful of where you walk, so as not to encroach on areas the Park rangers have designated as off-limits. As a national park, Mesa Verde receives between 400,000 to 600,000 visitors a year, so don't be surprised if you are sharing your favorite site with others who enjoy it just as much as you do. Explore, and most of all, appreciate the amazing job the Park Service has done in preserving this renowned World Heritage Site.

MESA VERDE
— A sunset or sunrise shoot at the Mancos Valley overlook may be a great place to start.

Instead of avoiding the denuded land by fire it is important to pay close attention to detail while interpreting change of the land, plants and wildlife in this arid climate caused by them through your lens.

Vistas from the North Rim can be spectacular especially in late spring where fog may stretch from the Montezuma Valley up the slopes of the mesa creating some unusual lighting and dramatic atmospheric conditions.

69 **Painted Wall–Black Canyon of the Gunnison**

Black Canyon of the Gunnison

On a bright afternoon looking west from the North Rim, you can see a ribbon of water shimmering 2,000 feet below before it disappears into the depths of darkness—this is the Black Canyon of the Gunnison. The walls are sheer, vertical, relentless and narrow. Over millions of years floodwaters from snowmelt and massive rains flowed freely through this canyon down the Gunnison River, carving it out of softer volcanic metamorphic at first, and harder igneous rock in layers further down.

In the past the inner gorge was unknown to all except for a few who dared to explore it; for us today, we know that Gunnison National Park was signed into law in 1933 by

President Herbert Hoover. Although the Black Canyon is 53 miles in length, 12 miles are designated as wilderness that can never be touched, protected by the Wilderness Act of 1964. Unseen are waters tapped as a resource flowing out of the canyon through a 5.8-mile irrigation tunnel to the Uncompahgre Valley. The canyon was mapped by Abraham Lincoln Fellows and William Torrence in 1901 for this singular purpose on a very risky exploratory venture down one of the steepest channels in the country—95 feet vertical drop per mile. (By comparison the Colorado River in the Grand Canyon drops, on average, about 27 vertical feet per mile.)

Lark Bunting

But one irrigation tunnel was not enough. Three man-made dams upstream of the canyon, built over the last century, have reduced the natural flow of the river to a trickle and the process of erosion in geologic terms has literally ground to a halt. If you take a moment to consider the impact of man's demand on the river in a scant 100 years, you can only wonder how long the wild indigenous creatures in this habitat can exist as they had. The next question is, "What will happen in the next 100 years if we continue to draw from the river as our growth continues unbridled?"

Regardless of its past and its future, photographing it from every possible angle, top to bottom and end to end, may help you understand the power of the Black Canyon of the Gunnison.

Photographing the Black Canyon of the Gunnison

Photographing the Black Canyon is very difficult. The depth, narrow width and near-vertical walls are the problems to work around and with. Sunlight does not touch the river and the top edge of the canyon simultaneously, except later in the morning until late in the afternoon. Unless you have an exceptional sunrise or sunset with tremendous lighting effect caused by some extensive atmospheric theatrics like a glowing, fiery sunset or sun filtering through sheets of rain as a squall passes to fill its walls top to bottom and a rainbow forms over the rim looking east to west, you are bound to be shooting at either edge in mid-morning or evening.

Choosing your location and looking for edges of land forms that accentuate posing light running along ridgelines against dark walls is one way to overcome this problem. Another is to work the Painted Wall, the tallest cliff in Colorado extending 2,250 feet from the river bottom to rim top. The pegmatite granite intrusion veins are a prominent feature of the Painted Wall. The three main minerals

71 **Fireweed on North Rim**

added to pegmatite are quartz, feldspar and mica. Apparently, this is the last water-saturated magma to cool, thus it becomes more fluid and easier to squeeze through cracks in the rock. It leaves an extensive mosaic pattern with crystals up to 6 feet in length as seen at the Painted Wall.

Another location of interest is the campsite at the east end of the Park below the crystal dam at the edge of the river. As the sun is catching the river at first or late light at the canyon bottom, it can create some interesting opportunities as you have the entire height of the walls to work with.

A wide angle lens 20 to 28mm would work well here. The fall is a good time to work the rim's edge and the colorful change of foliage on the plateau leading up to the edge. Making an exceptional photograph in the Black Canyon is rare, yet it's worth a few return trips once you have scouted out the place.

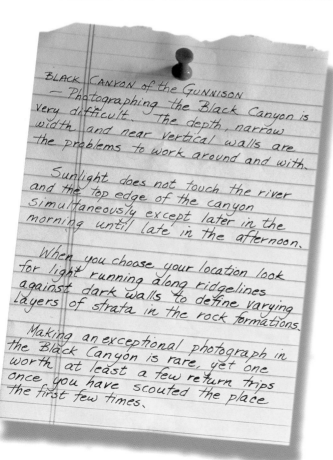

BLACK CANYON of the GUNNISON
— Photographing the Black Canyon is very difficult. The depth, narrow width and near vertical walls are the problems to work around and with.

Sunlight does not touch the river and the top edge of the canyon simultaneously except later in the morning until late in the afternoon.

When you choose your location look for light running along ridgelines against dark walls to define varying layers of strata in the rock formations.

Making an exceptional photograph in the Black Canyon is rare, yet one worth at least a few return trips once you have scouted the place the first few times.

72) Twilight Peak at Coal Bank Pass

San Juan Skyway

Of the many gorgeous roadside locales in Colorado, the San Juan Skyway ranks near the top—if not at the top—of the best places to photograph.

Not so long ago, roads blasted out of mountainsides climbing the heights of 12,000-foot-high passes carrying no more than a handful of stagecoach passengers were considered an engineering marvel and a novelty for those who could afford the fare. A stagecoach ride bore little if any resemblance to a luxury. Passengers sat squashed together next to and over stacks of mail; wore cloth masks to breathe, shielding their faces from the constant choke of dust; and endured rough hours on sparsely padded bench seats. Yet we still romantically fantasize about living in the Old Wild West. Today we drive smooth-riding air-conditioned vehicles that glide effortlessly over well-maintained paved roads curving around rocky mountain traverses we cannot fathom attempting on foot—then or now. We explore these places at our leisure in style without paying tribute to those who made it possible. Uncommon experiences for all but the rugged elite back then are possible for any one of us today. Scenic Byways, such as the San Juan Skyway, are a window of opportunity to explore the vast beauty and legendary heights of Colorado.

This paved stretch of road traverses some of Colorado's most rugged terrain. It links historic mining and supply towns together. Worn wood-boarded sidewalks on Main Street have given way to tourist friendly concrete-curbed architectural facades with well-preserved storefronts.

However, beyond the first steps through these doors, enough of the historic character has been saved to assure you a sense of those bygone days; you might even hear voices of the past calling to you. As one old man, an immigrant miner in his younger days, said in a deep, gruff voice bent by cigar smoke, "When you get to Tel-Lu-Ride, remember, say "hi" for me."

These voices call to women today as strongly as they did to men back then. Young women found in these resort towns are some of the strongest adventurers to take to the roads, guide the trails, drive livestock, run the rivers and climb the peaks—and they do it with gusto. For the native Ute and descendants of Ancient Puebloans, the voices speak another language from long ago: the voices of their ancestral grandmothers and grandfathers who summered in the high mountain meadows or clambered about their cliff dwellings.

The road is mapped and designated "San Juan Skyway." You will find it leads in many directions; most certainly, in ways you might not have expected, if you are open to it.

Sites and Photo Opportunities

Million Dollar Highway: Ouray to Silverton– Photographing in Ouray and its surrounding area is enticing in itself. In the winter there is the Box Canyon ice fall where ice climbers from around the world congregate each year; or you can photograph the ice falls themselves without climbers. In the summer, if you have a four-wheel-drive vehicle, head out of town on Forest Road 853 to Yankee Boy Basin or Imogene Pass for some great high peak vistas and wildflowers. There are many mining roads and miners' artifacts hereabouts. For some they are the attraction, an interesting part of history to photograph; for others they are distractions and cause for disappointment in having to work hard to find a pristine vista or angle without them in it. If you don't have a four-wheel-drive vehicle, you can commandeer a day trip from one of the companies in town offering excursions. No matter how you get here, this basin yields some of the most exceptional wildflower landscape photos anywhere.

About 10 miles south of Ouray are the Red Mountains and the

73 Ice formation at Box Canyon Falls

abandoned Irarado Mine. A large lumber trestle along the road remains from the mine's operational days and creates some interest in framing the mountains if there isn't much going on. However, if you take the time to climb the mountainside to the west of the highway about a quarter of a mile, your view of the Red Mountains, especially at sunset in summer or with patches of snow in late spring, can deliver a beautiful photograph. There are many opportunities roadside from Red Mountain Pass down to Silverton to capture images of the high peaks. Don't waste film here midday anytime of the year. Work this area for all it's worth when storms are brewing or just on their way out. The potential is excellent for great photographs.

Silverton is a historic gem. It sits at the end of the line for the narrow gauge out of Durango. Historic buildings downtown are tribute to its boom days as a Colorado mining powerhouse; try morning after sunrise or late afternoon through evening for exteriors. Keep your eyes open for happenings inside or interesting building interiors. There are many great vantages from the mountainside west of town to photograph the city at dawn with the iron-rich mountains behind them as a backdrop. The train pulls in and out of town daily. Compose the train tracks coming out of the bottom corners of the viewfinder with the train coming at you into town or going away during the evening.

74 Lone Pine on Red Mountain Pass

In mid to late June, the Animas River is at the height of the annual flood with rafters and kayakers flocking here to start their 25-mile run through the canyon alongside the narrow gauge tracks. You might find some good, rich colors with boaters' gear and spirited starts to their journeys. Any side trips out of town to the higher altitudes are a sure bet for interesting Colorado landscape vistas and grand views. Molas Pass and Coal Bank Pass on the road from Silverton to Durango offer superb turnouts to capture shots of the Grenadier Range, Engineer Mountain and Twilight Peak in the West Needles Mountains. You may even want to take a day hike on the Colorado Trail atop Molas Pass. If you drive about a half mile on a dirt road to the west just off the top of Molas Pass on the north side, you find Little Molas Lake and some great evening reflections of Snowdon Peak.

Durango–The old iron engine puffs coal smoke into the air as passengers scramble into train cars to the cry from the engineers, "All Aboard!" The whistle blows as throngs watch, some photographing the narrow gauge train as it leaves the station in Durango on its daily summer scheduled run to Silverton and back. The Durango Silverton narrow gauge train is one of this region's major attractions. Plan a full day for the ride and time to explore Silverton on either side of the trip. In town photograph the train after it crosses 15th Street on the bridge over the Animas River on its way to Silverton. Along Highway 550, set up slightly away from the tracks with a mountain scene as the backdrop, eliminating contemporary buildings yet including his-

75 **Durango and Silverton narrow gauge train**

torical buildings as the train passes. About 14 miles north of town on Highway 550, take a right into Rockwood on Secondary Forest Route 745 about 2 miles to the winter turn-around and terminal for the train; this is a great place to get a shot before the train disappears into the Animas River Canyon. Fort Lewis College sits atop a butte on the east edge of town where you can find landscape images of the city with the La Plata Mountains to the west. The Animas River flows through town where there are more than a handful of possibilities to catch fly fisherman and river runners enjoying their favorite pastimes.

Cortez to Telluride–As you leave the Cortez area and travel Route 145 to Telluride, you cannot help but notice that this is one of the most famous places in the state to photograph each fall. You climb from high desert to the heights of the San Juans along the Dolores River through Rico and over Lizard Head Pass at 10,222 feet to the Ophir Loop. Just after you drop off the pass toward Ophir, you will find Trout Lake; it won't take you long to figure this is photographed best in the evening. A short drive up the Ophir Loop and you come to abandoned mine shafts that

define this valley as much as the mountainsides on which they sit. Along Route 145 from Ophir Loop to Telluride, there are grand vistas of Mount Wilson (14, 245 feet) and El Diente Peak (14,159 feet). Mornings are memorable and significant for photographs from this location, especially with fall colors and snow on the peaks or early summer with wildflowers. Once you have arrived in Telluride, you can find your way to Bridal Veil Falls and hike to Blue Lake. There is the traditional shot from the main street in town with Ajax Peak in the background. An evening atop Telluride Ski Area at the Gondola Terminal for a sunset view of the Sneffels Range is a worthwhile venture if you have the time.

Dallas Divide to Ridgeway–Highway 62 runs through Pleasant Valley West of Ridgeway up a long grade to the Dallas Divide, all the while the magnificent Sneffels Range dominates the view to the south. Great photographs of this formidable landscape are the standards against which fall Colorado photographs are judged. There are a couple of unpaved roads leading to the edge of the wilderness off Highway 62 to the south that can lead you to exceptional locations. Try East Dallas Road or County Road 7 about 4 miles west of Ridgeway, or about three-quarters of a mile west is West Dallas Road or County Road 9. Four-wheel drive is not

76) **Little Molas Lake on Molas Pass**

turnouts and opportunities for great landscape photographs. A classic one is the cross-hatched fence line running from the foreground of the photograph into the distance with the Sneffels Range as a backdrop and a beautiful sunset. There is another preferable location on the south side of the valley on County Road 1 that winds up a steep paved grade to Log Hill Mesa. Take Highway 550 north from Ridgeway to County Road 24, turn left or west and go about 3.5 miles to County Road 1, turn right and follow it up the hill until you find the immense view across the valley to the Sneffels Range. These

required but having it certainly won't deter your efforts, especially on wet, muddy or snowpacked roads. Work away from the road, taking short walks to elevated ridges or hillsides for vistas without too much clutter in the foreground. Along Highway 62 all the way up to the Divide, there are a number of

77) **Red Mountain Pass**

locations are great in the morning or evening. Don't pass through this magnificent area too quickly; stay a few days to catch it just right.

SAN JUAN SCENIC SKYWAY
~ Of the many gorgeous roadside locales in Colorado, the San Juan Skyway ranks near the top - if not at the top - of the best places to photograph.

In the summer, if you have a four-wheel-drive vehicle, head out of town on Forest Road 853 to Yankee Boy Basin or Imogene Pass for some great high peak vistas and wildflowers.

Silverton is a historic gem. It sits at the end of the line for the narrow gauge out of Durango. There are many great vantages from the mountainside west of town to photograph the city at dawn with the iron-rich mountains behind them as a backdrop.

78 **Owl Creek Pass**

Owl Creek Pass

The Cimarron Road south off Colorado Highway 50 leading up to Owl Creek Pass offers little advance notice of what lies ahead, yet it may be the most interesting way to begin your excursion. By comparison, Highway 550, with its sweeping vistas of the spectacular crags near Courthouse Mountain, gives you every indication of what's in store for miles in advance. Either way you drive into the area, these well-main-tained unpaved roads deliver you to the heart of the Uncompahgre National Forest and to the edge of the Uncompahgre Wilderness. Here you'll find some of the most exceptional volcanic formations, mountains and land-scapes in all of Colorado. Sweeping, undulating valleys filled with lakes, streams, meadows, endless stands of quaking aspen and jagged ridgelines with unusual spires (known as chimneys and pipes)

79 **West Fork of the Cimarron**

assure that you have arrived. This area show-cases the role explosive volcanic action has played in creating the San Juan Mountains over the past 65 million years. Combine the volcanism with the powerful erosive forces of wind, water and ice, and you have an idea of how this place came into being. Owl Creek Pass isn't just another great scenic Colorado Byway. It is one of those places away from it all that is well worth the turn down the road less traveled.

Photographing Owl Creek Pass

You may want to be here at the height of the wildflower blooming season in early to mid July, or come again in the fall in late September or early October. You don't have to stray far from the roadway for great photographs. Take just a step or two out of your way, and you will be rewarded with unique angles and perspectives. Consider staying for three to five days to catch just the right shot at the right moment. It is recommended that you take a day to familiarize yourself with the topography once you've arrived. Remember to research your locations and note the time of day to position yourself for the best light, morning or evening. If you get off the main road, you will need a regional topographical map of the area to know where the four-wheel-drive roads

80 **Reflection on Silver Jack Reservoir**

and side hikes lead you. A Colorado atlas and gazetteer is a great tool in preparing for a trip into this area.

Silver Jack Reservoir

There is a stunning view with a reflection on the lake just down the hill from the campground at Silver Jack Reservoir at the edge of the dam looking south across the lake. Choose a calm morning or evening with some high, striated lenticular clouds for best results. At the south end of

81 **Fenceline on Owl Creek Pass**

the lake, three volcanically sculpted valleys and tributaries from the West, Middle and East Forks of the Cimarron River intersect to create this grand view.

West, Middle and East Forks of the Cimarron River

Any one of the three forks of the Cimarron River offer great photographic opportunities. The rivers and meadows provide strong bases or anchors to build the composition of your photograph. Each valley

75

82 Aspen grove on Owl Creek Pass

offers vistas of massive mountainous formations in the background. Lower in the valleys you'll find exquisite stands of aspen and pine forests higher up. If you don't have a four-wheel-drive vehicle, you may need to walk or hike. Look for clearings from the valley looking up or find a perch on a mountainside looking down and across for the best angles. West Fork offers some of the highest peaks with truly unique shapes—Dunsinane Mountain, Precipice Peak, Courthouse Mountain, Redcliff and Coxcomb Peak.

83 Spire on Owl Creek Pass

ridgelines, using a long focal length lens of 180mm or greater. Use a wide angle lens to capture a field of wildflowers set beneath the peaks as an evening thunderstorm clears. Once you cross over Owl Creek Pass driving west toward Ridgeway, you'll have extensive views looking east toward Courthouse Mountain and southwest toward the Sneffels Range and Pleasant Valley. You may have to work for a perspective from higher ground than the roadway.

Owl Creek Pass Road

Just north of Silver Jack Reservoir, there is a four-wheel-drive road to a small beaver dam with a beautiful stand of huge aspen and a cragged ridgeline in the background. Drive south from Silver Jack Reservoir on Owl Creek Pass Road to find a number of potential locations. Work the Cimarron as it flows into Silver Jack Reservoir and a small lake. The aspen stands create a number of opportunities to study light playing in and amongst them. Look for elevated locations compressing the foreground with aspen and the background with high

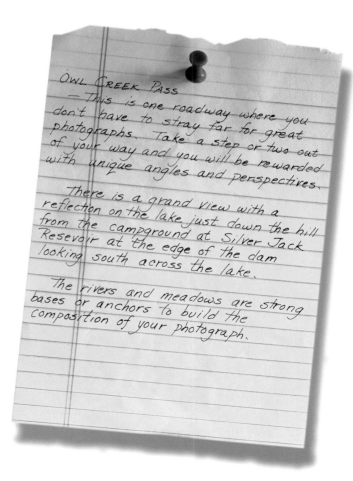

OWL CREEK PASS
— This is one roadway where you don't have to stray far for great photographs. Take a step or two out of your way and you will be rewarded with unique angles and perspectives.

There is a grand view with a reflection on the lake just down the hill from the campground at Silver Jack Resevoir at the edge of the dam looking south across the lake.

The rivers and meadows are strong bases or anchors to build the composition of your photograph.

Porcupine

Royal Gorge

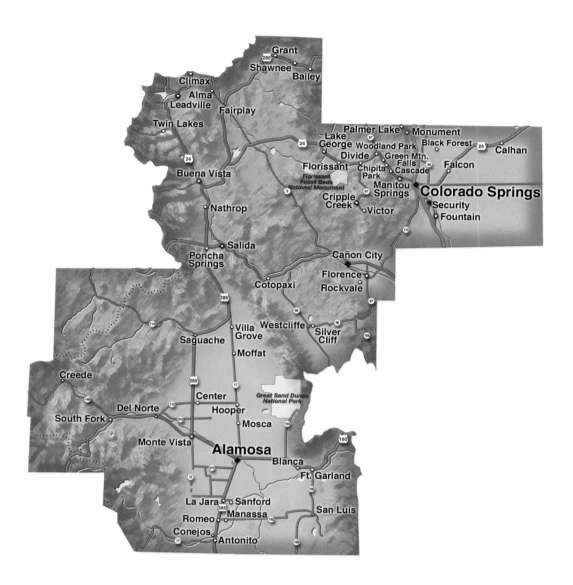

THE South Central
R E G I O N

The South Central Region defines the state of Colorado as much as it is a place in the state. This area is everything Colorado was 20 years ago; somehow it has missed the recent rush to develop every last spot on the map. Here you feel the land and how it has shaped the people and, in turn, how they have shaped the land. This is Colorado's "Big Sky Country."

Not only is it the great wide-open spaces that capture your imagination as you drive through its vastness, but it's also the raw sense of power nature holds in this area and our part in it that makes it special. As you drive the roads in the South Central Region, observe it with a keen sense of its scale, and explore it with the sense of urgency that is moving many to preserve nature's remaining pristine gifts before they disappear.

The South Central quietly boasts some of the biggest, highest, original, and best of everything found in Colorado. To start, the

85) **Monte Vista Wildlife Refuge**

wide-open San Luis Valley sweeps up to the heights of the jagged-edge Sangre de Cristo Mountains. The region is home to the head-waters of the Arkansas River—one of the country's most popular and technical whitewater rivers. *Outdoor* magazine named Salida one of

86) **Columbia Peak—The Collegiate Range**

the most livable cities for outdoor enthusiasts in the United States. At 10,300 feet, Leadville sits among the tallest peaks in the state as the highest city in the nation. More 14,000-foot

peaks rise to the heights of the Continental Divide in this region than any other in the state, and it is home to the highest—Mount Elbert at 14,333 feet. Great Sand Dunes National Monument and Preserve, the Wheeler Geologic Area, Slumgollion Pass, South Park and the Garden of the Gods are some of the most beautiful, unique and inter-esting geologic phenomena to be found any-where in Colorado. The Cumbres & Toltec Scenic Railroad, a National and State Registered Historic Site, is America's longest and highest narrow gauge railroad. Each spring and fall sandhill and whooping cranes, among the world's largest birds, fly their ancient migratory routes north and south through the magnificent Alamosa and Monte Vista Wildlife Refuges. Our country's best ath-letes, even the best in the world, train at the U.S. Olympic Training Center in Colorado Springs. Among the quietest places to ski are the slopes at Wolf Creek Ski Area, and the most hardy souls snowshoe atop Wolf Creek Pass.

The real gems, however, are the off-the-beaten path places rarely visited that can be found in the La Garita, Sangre de Cristo, South San Juan and Weminuche Wildernesses. When someone asks where you go to get away from Colorado's madding crowd, be quiet. Don't tell them you know the best-kept local secrets in Colorado are right here in the South Central Region.

Red Tail Hawk

87 Hoodoos–Wheeler Geologic Area

Wheeler Geologic Area

Wheeler Geologic Area is a remote geologic conglomeration of exquisite volcanic formations found just northeast of the historic mining town of Creede. The raw effects of wind, water and ice eroding massive deposits of fine-grained particles of volcanic dust known as "tuft" over more than 65 million years created this site. The white, grey, buff-colored Rat Creek Tuft reminds people of South Dakota's Badlands. Irregular-shaped formations known as Hoodoos along with spires, broken ridges, fluted walls and columns dominate the main group of formations that are almost gothic in their design. Not only does

the Wheeler Geologic Area have an interesting geologic history, it also has an illustrious past. It was designated as a national monument by Theodore Roosevelt in 1908 through the Antiquities Act of 1906. Originally it was named the Wheeler National Monument after Lieutenant George M. Wheeler of the U.S. Army Corps of Topographical Engineers who worked this region of Colorado in 1874. The monument did not survive though, as it was difficult to get to, remote and never actually funded. Its status as a national monument was terminated and the land was transferred to the Forest Service in 1950, with the local

88 Sunset–Wheeler Geologic Area

populace supporting the move to keep it a public entity. During the 1960s a logging road increased traffic to the site. The *Denver Post* decried these actions as outrageous and the general public reacted accordingly. On September 11, 1969, the site was closed at Wheeler and the surrounding area by the Forest Service. Conservation groups viewed the defects of the site (inaccessible with low patronage) as virtues, supporting the idea that the area be moved into the La Garita Wilderness; this proposal died in Congress. Today the entrance to the area is fenced, and a walking path circumnavigates the site. The Rio Grande National Forest has done an outstanding job in providing excellent interpretive signage at its entrance. More people than ever make the difficult excursion to one of the little-known wonders of Colorado's landscape, and it is well worth the effort.

Photographing Wheeler Geologic Area

This is one of the most remote and difficult places to get to in Colorado. It is an arduous two and a half hour four-wheel-drive adventure or the intermediate 7-mile one-way hike. It is not open in winter and closed until late spring. Check with the Rio Grande Forest Service office in Creede before heading out. To get there take Highway 149 approximately 13 miles west of South Fork to Pool Table Mountain Turnoff (FSR 600). Travel another 13 miles to the Hanson's Mill site. From here you can hike 7 miles or drive 14 miles on an unimproved rugged two-track road. Don't expect to drive more than 5 miles an hour—this is true for the most experienced four-wheel enthusiast. Once you reach the end of the road, there is a 2.5-mile trail that loops around the area, and it is a half-mile uphill hike to the first open vantage point on the west side of the area.

Photographing the Wheeler area is best at first light in the morning or late in the evening. The traditional view of the area is from the west edge about a half mile up the trail from the end of the road. In the morning the sun has to climb above a ridge 1,500 feet above the formations to the east so they are obstructed for at least 45 minutes to an hour after sunrise. It might take some brightly lit high cumulus or lenticular cirrus clouds to provide

enough fill light bouncing off their ceiling to make this shot worth taking. Nonetheless it is well worth waking before dawn

Black Bear

to get on the path to your location. The evening presents a different set of lighting situations with the potential for an evening thunderstorm or unusual cloud formations to set up. One of the better locations is on top of the northwest ridge where there are rolling tuft mounds with the Hoodoos and the mountain ridgeline off in the distance. Taking the time to walk around the site navigating your search for interesting locations will serve you well when it comes time to shoot. Since you may be here for an afternoon and evening or one overnighter, you have to work with light you get and even if it isn't the most desirable, you will not go away empty-handed.

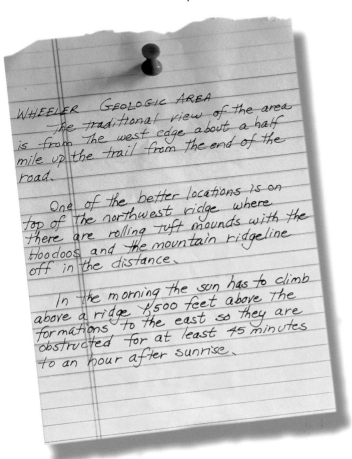

WHEELER GEOLOGIC AREA
The traditional view of the area is from the west edge about a half mile up the trail from the end of the road.

One of the better locations is on top of the northwest ridge where there are rolling tuft mounds with the Hoodoos and the mountain ridgeline off in the distance.

In the morning the sun has to climb above a ridge 1,500 feet above the formations to the east so they are obstructed for at least 45 minutes to an hour after sunrise.

89 The Collegiate Range and the Upper Arkansas River Valley

The Upper Arkansas River Valley

The Upper Arkansas River Valley is home to one of Colorado's most storied historical mining towns, Leadville, and the start of one of the most exciting white-water rivers in North America. The glacially carved valley is paralleled by two mountain ranges running north and south. The Sawatch Mountains are on the west side, and the Arkansas Hills at the southern tail of the Mosquito Range are on the east side of the valley. The Sawatch Mountains are home to the Collegiate Range and 15 peaks above 14,000 feet. Although the mountains to the west receive more than 100 inches of snowfall in an average year, the

90 Kayaking the Numbers–The Arkansas River

hills to the east receive half as much. All the snowmelt from these peaks feeds the Arkansas River, one of Colorado's most popular summer destinations for whitewater rafting and kayaking. At the uppermost reaches of the head-

waters is Leadville, the highest city in the United States, and 52 miles downstream is Salida, proclaimed one of the most livable cities in the nation. Along the Arkansas River corridor between the two cities lie some of the most fabled rapids in the West, including the Numbers, the Narrows, Browns Canyon, and below Salida toward Pueblo, the Gorge. Commercial river guides provide trips from a

half day to multiple days. There is no shortage of professionals to assure you a safe, exciting day on the river. If you are not into whitewater, there is camping, hiking, fishing, mountain biking and climbing. To soothe your muscles after a day out in the high country, you may want to drop into Mount Princeton or Cottonwood Hot Springs. Beyond the recreational opportunities, this is a beautiful valley with mountains rising 4,000 feet from the valley floor. This is where the photographers test their abilities making photographs as much as the outdoor enthusiasts climbing the peaks test their skills.

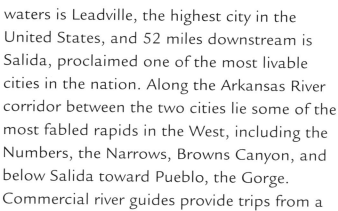

UPPER ARKANSAS RIVER VALLEY
One great location to photograph the entire Collegiate Range with an unobstructed vista is from the Arkansas hills.

Down along the river at any number of locations, photographing kayakers and rafters makes for excellent outdoor action images.

If you are looking for high-peak vistas, take a shot at climbing one of the Fourteeners ... Atop these peaks are expansive vistas of endless mountains north, south, and west.

Photographing the Upper Arkansas River Valley

To get to the Arkansas River Valley from Denver take one of two routes. Go west on I-70 to Copper Mountain and exit onto Highway 91, and head south by west to Leadville to Highway 24, which turns into Highway 285 at Johnsons Corner just below Buena Vista and runs through Salida to Pueblo. The second and quickest route from Denver is taking Highway 285 from the Conifer/Bailey Exit of C-470 with a scenic two-and-three-quarter-hour drive through South Park to Buena Vista.

Scenic landscape images are a staple for any photographer working this area as the beauty of the Rocky Mountains sings loud and strong. One great location to photograph the entire Collegiate Range with an unobstructed vista is from the Arkansas Hills. To

92 **Fourteeners: Little Bear, Ellingwood Point, Blanca Peak and Mount Lindsey– The Sangre de Cristos**

get to this location, turn south off Highway 285 (5 miles east of Johnsons Corner) on Forest Road 315 and drive 2 miles up Shield Gulch until you reach the ridge where you have a magnificent vantage point for photographing. Photographing the Collegiate Range looking up from the valley floor from County Road 162 heading west from Nathrop to the Mount Princeton Hot Springs gives a perspective of how tall these peaks really stand.

Down along the river at any number of locations, photographing kayakers and rafters makes for excellent outdoor action images. An outstanding place to start along the river is at the Chaffee County Road 371 Bridge that crosses the Arkansas River at Rapid V on the Numbers. Take Highway 24 8 miles north of Buena Vista and turn right on Road 371; go about a half mile to the river and wait for kayakers and rafters. Mid to late morning is the best time for activity on this stretch of the river. Head south on Road 371 as it parallels the river to

Elephant Rock; stop along the road, then find a perch overlooking Frog Rock Rapid for some whitewater action. If you are looking for high-peak vistas, take a shot at climbing one of the Fourteeners; make sure you start before or at sunrise to avoid getting caught in a thunderstorm. Atop these peaks are expansive vistas of endless mountains north, south and west. If you happen to be on top with some billowy

93 **Owl on old barn--San Luis Valley**

cumulus clouds and broken morning light, all the better. Be prepared for rain or possibly snow, and moving off these mountains quickly if need be. There are hundreds of roads and vistas; it's up to you to choose the one with the best vista and available evening or morning light.

Cutthroat Trout

94 Ripples at sunrise on the Dunefield

The Great Sand Dunes National Monument and Preserve

They appear magically, looming large, far off in the distance, almost as if this is the other side of the planet—like the Sahara of Africa. Set mysteriously below high peaks of the Sangre de Cristo Mountains, rolling sand dunes rise out of the San Luis Valley as if they were placed there as one of nature's afterthoughts. In fact the dunes play an important part in a set of highly evolved interdependent ecosystems known as life zones. The most visible and easily distinguishable is the Dunefield because of its height and breadth. It measures just 30 square miles and, oddly enough, it is the smallest sand deposit of the Great Sand Dunes system. All told it holds approximately 4.8 billion cubic feet of eolian sand. When compared to its sandy neighbors, the Sand Sheet just west of the Dunefield, which measures 180 square miles, and farther west into the valley near the San Luis Lakes, the Sabhka, which measures 120 square miles, the Dunefield is a fraction of the whole system's size. The Sand Sheet is almost entirely sand with a fair amount of vegetation holding the sand in place, and it is mostly flat except for some small hills and depressions. The Sabhka is sand cemented by highly concentrated alkaline and mineral rich water; when it dries, it creates a fragile crust making for a landscape that appears baked and barren. The underlying mixture of sand and water below the crust is soft and unstable, making it unsuitable for building. With the soil so alkaline, it is impossible for plants to gain a foothold and so, it's not suitable for farming. But it is the Dunefield that draws us inside the preserve's

95 Sunflowers in August– the Dunefield

boundary to learn and to play.

Through the ages sand dunes were formed with sand blown by strong northeasterly winds funneling over Medano and Mosca Passes, then deposited in the basin below. Wind continues to work the dunes, constantly changing their shape, form and size. There are five different shapes of dunes—Star, Parabolic, Transvers, Barchan and Reversing Dunes. Each form is developed through specific wind patterns that create a unique design. How many can you identify while you are here? A hike to the top of the dunes some 450 feet above the valley floor gives you a view of the fields of sand that appear to stretch endlessly to the mountains and the Sand Sheet and Sabhka to the west. Atop the dunes your perspective of their size and forms is altered considerably, compared to standing below them at Medano Creek looking up.

Just as it is for people, water is the lifeblood of the sand dunes; it is water that holds this complex system together. The water filtering through the sand is some of the purest found anywhere. Water is the glue that holds the dunes in places and acts as a recycling system. Each spring the water flows through Medano Creek from May to August during years with average or better snowfall. Two unusual characteristics of Medano Creek are its mysterious pulses, and the fact that its flow decreases during the day. The pulsing action occurs when small sand dams are creat-

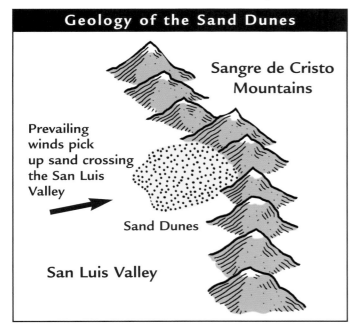

Geology of the Sand Dunes

Sangre de Cristo Mountains

Prevailing winds pick up sand crossing the San Luis Valley

Sand Dunes

San Luis Valley

ed upstream by spring runoff then broken by the surges in the flow, creating mini-waves that sweep down the creek. Another factor in the streams are the huge cottonwoods that line the creek to the south. They drink heavily from the creek as the sun hits the leaves of the trees, increasing the rate of photosynthesis and the need for water to sustain the process. Oddly enough, the flow of the creek increases at night and decreases during the day. During the worst drought conditions, such as those of 2002, the flow in Medano Creek does not appear at all.

Although Medano Creek is easiest to experience firsthand because it is so close to the Dunefield parking lot, it is just one part of the water story here. Each spring, snowmelts from the high alpine and subalpine life zones cascade into lakes at timberline. The water flows through forests of fir and spruce, beaver ponds lined by mountain wildflowers, extensive aspen and cottonwood groves and finally into the ponderosa forest; then apparently it disappears in the Dunefield only to reappear to the west in ponds in the Sand Sheet and Sabhka life zones. Up until the 1940s there were more than 80 ponds in the wetlands west of the Dunefield. The pond numbers have dwindled to five, due to an apparent increase in demand for water from the San Luis Valley Aquifer for irrigation and for cities. If the water table drops too far, the ponds will evaporate entirely, laying this area to waste. Besides the people downstream, a wide range

of plants, insects and wildlife are dependent on water flowing into and around the dunes. A number of unique insects, beetles, crickets, moths and flies, are found only at the Great Sand Dunes National Monument and Preserve. It is usually easier to find their tracks in the sand than it is to find them. In wetter years, sunflowers bloom, creating a beautiful trail of green and yellow, following the curving V-shaped valleys between the dunes. Herds of deer graze in the low-lying bush in the evenings or take a sip of water from the creek. Birds of prey soar high above, and then land for a drink. There are horned lizards, jackrabbits, Ord's kangaroo rats and coyotes aplenty. Water is everything to the dunes and all its inhabitants in the natural circle of life. It is our connection to this place as human beings that makes us wonder about those who walked here before us. Long ago, Native people (Jicarilla Apache, Tewa Pueblo and Ute) who inhabited the San Luis Valley came here to gather sand for their paintings,

Mule Deer Buck

97 The Dunefield and Sangre de Cristo Mountains

possibly to hunt and seek water. Today there is a spiritual component for Jicarilla Apache who collect sand here and carry on the age-old tradition of their ancestors in making sand paintings. Natives had to give way to the pressures of the Europeans and later Euro-Americans. Spanish explorers and settlers made their way into this valley as early as the mid-1500s. The rush for gold in the West took place in the late 1850s; unsuccessful gold seekers turned to farming as they found the valley well suited to agriculture with the abundance of spring and river water. We owe a debt to those whose efforts to preserve this area resulted in the creation of a national monument in 1932 and later, Great Sand Dunes National Monument and Preserve. They helped ensure that future generations of Americans will find it as the Natives did

thousands of years ago—wild and pristine.

Photographing the Great Sand Dunes

The Dunefield offers a phenomenal opportunity to photograph and explore its expanse. To get here take Highway 17 to Road 6N then head due east to the dunes and mountains, where you will find the park entrance and visitors center. Along the way you will find San Luis State Park and San Luis Lake. The lake is a good location for an evening sunset shot with the dunes and mountains in the reflection across the water's surface. The dunes are best photographed at first or last light of day. Weather changes provide dramatic atmospheric conditions to enhance your chances of making extraordinary photographs. On their way to the monument, storms often move in the large opening created by the San Luis Valley to the west. Summer thunderstorms and winter snow squalls are backlit by late rays of sun stretching from the far west above the San Juan Mountains, creating great shadows and high-

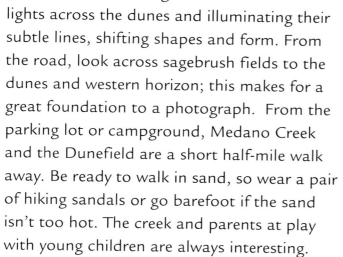

lights across the dunes and illuminating their subtle lines, shifting shapes and form. From the road, look across sagebrush fields to the dunes and western horizon; this makes for a great foundation to a photograph. From the parking lot or campground, Medano Creek and the Dunefield are a short half-mile walk away. Be ready to walk in sand, so wear a pair of hiking sandals or go barefoot if the sand isn't too hot. The creek and parents at play with young children are always interesting.

Yet it is the hike to the top of the dunes and beyond that will yield the most notable images. Make sure your camera gear is well protected so sand does not get in the lenses or the camera body; it only takes a grain or two to do irreparable damage to your gear, and possibly, scratch your film. Once on top or in the dunes, the possibilities for great shots can be overwhelming. Choose a number of angles from one location per sunrise or sunset and hold the ones you missed for the next session. Concentrate on the dunes' form, sand texture and shape. Work on compressing the foreground filled with the dunes and the background with the mountains and sky while keeping them all in focus. You can make this process easier by positioning yourself on top of a dune that is higher and overlooking a valley to the top of the next one and those

98 **Beetle tracks on the Dunefield**

beyond it. Look for vegetation, placing it in the picture as the subject with the surrounding dunes cradling them. Don't be too surprised to find insect or snake tracks in the sand— they are excellent close-up subjects against the texture of the fine grain sand.

Try capturing people skiing, snowboarding or running down the dunes kicking up sand that is backlit as it sprays in their wake. You may even include footprints disappearing into the distance and covered by windblown sand to create interest and scale. One rule the park rangers encourage you to remember is this: Never alter any natural object or living creature to attain your desired photograph.

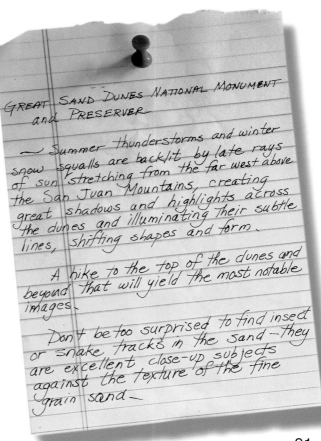

GREAT SAND DUNES NATIONAL MONUMENT and PRESERVER

~ Summer thunderstorms and winter snow squalls are backlit by late rays of sun stretching from the far west above the San Juan Mountains, creating great shadows and highlights across the dunes and illuminating their subtle lines, shifting shapes and form.

A hike to the top of the dunes and beyond that will yield the most notable images.

Don't be too surprised to find insect or snake tracks in the sand—they are excellent close-up subjects against the texture of the fine grain sand—

99 Garden of the Gods

Garden of the Gods

The Legend
Beyond the Name

The rare, red fins of the Fountain Formation are found along the Front Range from Boulder to Colorado Springs. The most inspirational, though, is the group near Colorado Springs named by a young surveyor in 1859 when a poetic Rufus Cable proclaimed, "Why it is a fitting place for the Gods to assemble. We will call it the Garden of the Gods." This was in response to the other surveyor who suggested this would be "a capital place for a beer garden." To this day the park is open to the public with many wonderful walking trails meandering in and around its unique formations. Their

names, Balanced Rock, Kissing Camels and Siamese Twins, are legendary.

There is a Native American legend about how Garden of the Gods came to be, written by Ford C. Frick and on file at the Pioneers Museum in Colorado Springs: "In the nestling vales and on the grassy plains which lie at the foot of the Great White Mountain that points the way to heaven lived the Chosen People. Here they dwelt in happiness together. And above them on the summit of the Mighty Peak where stand the Western Gates of Heaven, dwelt the Manitou. And that the Chosen People might know of his love the Manitou did stamp upon the Peak the image of his face that all might see and worship him ... But one day as the storm clouds played about the Peak, the image of the Manitou was hid ... Then came to pass a wondrous miracle. The clouds broke away and sunshine smote the Peak, and from the very summit, looking down, appeared the face of Manitou himself. And stern he looked upon the advancing host, and as he looked the Giants and the beasts turned into stone within their very steps ... And when the white men came they called the spot the Garden of the Gods ... but we who know the history of the race still call it *Valley of the Miracle*, for here it was that Manitou gave aid to save his chosen people." No doubt Garden of the Gods will speak to you as surely as it has to all those who have walked here before you.

Photographing Garden of the Gods

Directions to the North Entrance. Take I-25 to Garden of the Gods Road at Exit 146, go west to 30th Street and turn left or south, then drive to the North Entrance of the park.

100 **Fountain formation sunlit through morning fog**

The Fountain Formations that dominate this valley, the rolling hills immediately to the west and farther in the distance to the west, Pikes Peak, all make the Garden of the Gods ideal to photograph early in the morning. Exceptional weather conditions, such as an upslope spring snowstorm fading to the east as the sun rises or a low-lying rainstorm clearing from the valley and peaks behind, enhance your chances for a great photograph. Garden of the Gods, like all locations, deserves the time it takes in the afternoon or evening before you photograph to walk and know as much about the potential locations to shoot from as possible. Study the Balanced Rock, the Kissing Camels and the varying formations with an eye for how the light will play off of them from a number of angles. At sunrise these Formations radiate a heavenly orange-red glow that few of the formations along the Front Range exhibit, making them enchanting to photograph.

Garden of the Gods Geology

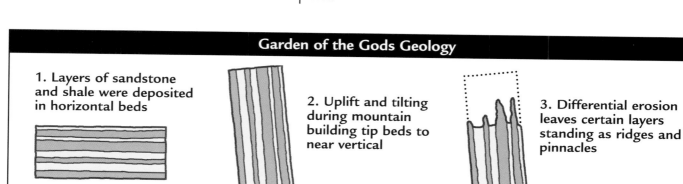

1. Layers of sandstone and shale were deposited in horizontal beds

2. Uplift and tilting during mountain building tip beds to near vertical

3. Differential erosion leaves certain layers standing as ridges and pinnacles

Civic Center Park

THE CITY OF
Denver

Born out of the harsh arid Western landscape, Denver sits on the edge of the Great Plains at the foot of the Rocky Mountains, 30 miles east of the heights of the Continental Divide at the center of the United States. Founded November 22, 1858, and incorporated November 7, 1861, Denver is the capital of Colorado. Although Denver was diplomatically named after Territorial Governor James Denver, General William H. Larimer named its major street for himself. Today, it is home to more than 506,250 people who inhabit 154.63 square miles at 5,280 feet above sea level. The South Platte is the

102 Colorado State Capitol

103 Union Station and night skyline

major river flowing through downtown along with its smaller tributaries Cherry Creek and Sand Creek.

With more than 300 days of sunshine per year, Denver's average February temperature is 33 degrees and the average August temperature is 72 degrees. The city receives about 55 inches of snow and 15 inches of rain a year. The city boasts 285 city parks covering 4,508 acres of land, and 13,600 acres of mountain parks. There are 97 miles of parkway and 125 miles of hike/bikeways. It has 34 sculpted fountains, including an interactive fountain at City Park. Culturally, it has the second-largest performing arts complex in the contiguous United States. Denver is home to the 17,000-acre wildlife habitat at Rocky Mountain Arsenal, a rare environmental oasis and preserve set among urban sprawl and development. It can even claim the only noxious weed-eating goat herd in the country.

Inner City Fox

Its proximity to the mountains, diversity of culture and quality of life combine to make living in the Mile High City truly a magical experience.

Native and Euro-American History

A little more than 145 years ago, neither the state of Colorado nor Denver City existed. This place was wild, considered an inhospitable high plains desert, unknown to all but a few Anglo-Europeans. Arapaho, Cheyenne and a few trappers and frontiersmen were the only ones to inhabit the area from the early to mid-1800s. The Arapaho lodges spread out in a village on the west and east banks of Cherry Creek at its confluence with the South Platte. The land was rich in natural beauty and filled with a plethora of wildlife. The Native people settled along the free-flowing creeks and rivers where water was easy to get, and crops easy to grow. They hunted wild bison, deer, antelope, elk and foraged for and made medicine from natural plants in the region. The Arapaho and Cheyenne adapted well to life on the plains beneath the high peaks of the Rockies.

Considering Denver as the gateway to the West is not a new idea. Boosters in the late 1870s to 1880s who envisioned the "Queen City" of the high plains as the Gateway to the Rockies deserve credit. They lobbied Washington for the right to "designate Denver as an official port of entry." Denver was awarded a customs house in 1882 instead. Regardless of its conditional standing with Washington, Denver promoters foretold its future with the vision for the city as an international hub of transportation and business. The Welcome Arch, a monumental structure at Wynkoop and 18th Streets at Union Station, erected by Mayor Speer with private funding in July 1906, may have been built to further cement this concept. Historian and author Tom Noel writes, "Mayor Speer dedicated the arch ... declaring that it is to stand here for the ages as an expression of love, good wishes and kind feelings of our citizens to the stranger who enters our gates.'" However, the promoters' vision took a little longer to materialize than they had originally planned. Denver's dreams of being an international port had to wait, even though the idea burned strong until the 1980s.

Long before Denver was touted as an official port of entry, it attracted people who arrived by simpler means of travel. As the Western frontier opened, frontiersmen, trappers, settlers and gold seekers rode horses, drove Conestoga or farm wagons, pulled carts and walked on foot. Crossing

104 Fountain at entrance to City Park

the plains was a risky proposition at best, and the consequences were severe for the less fortunate. The routes were long, rough and dusty for what must have seemed to the travelers as an endless stretch across the Midwestern plains. The early route was the legendary Oregon Trail to the Ash Hollow crossing of the South Platte on to Julesburg to Fort Morgan then into Denver. The journey to Denver was about 600 miles from Independence, Missouri, and the trip could take 60 to 75 days depending on conditions. One in ten died attempting to make their way across the plains. The prospects of finding the good life at the end of the trail were slim. Denver was described by an early visitor as "a huddle of log cabins with every other building a saloon." Nonetheless, the march west was on, whether by foot or other mode of transport.

Parks, Arts and Architecture

Denver is renowned for its parks, museums and world-class attractions, which give an added dimension to the Mile High City's character. They provide lifelong learning opportunities for young and old alike, but they also give people a chance to let it all go and have some fun. The variety is a tribute to the visionaries and creators who have brought them to life. Wherever you go in Denver, there is a sense of pride in how caretakers,

105 **Moonset at sunrise over Denver skyline**

volunteers and administrators tend to these special places. More than just welcome escapes from the ordinary, they are a delight for all who dare venture one step beyond the comforts of the everyday world and let their imaginations soar.

Denver has fast developed an international reputation as a center for the arts. At first, you might think of the world-renowned Denver Performing Arts Complex with its jam-packed schedule of Broadway shows and performances. Or maybe the exotic Denver Art Museum, designed by the Milanese architect Gio Ponti, and home to a myriad of highly acclaimed permanent and touring exhibits. Look again and you will find there are many more treasures around Denver in the most unusual places. Art crosses cultural lines, ages and classes, lending perspective to spaces and leading you to ask, "What if?" In Denver the questions are: "What works, and how can we?" Art and the performing arts are indelibly etched into and celebrated in Denver's cultural landscape. The arts breathe life into the city, and energize her people. It is no small coincidence that the arts thrive in Denver as no place else in the West.

In her 145 short years of existence, Denver's architecture has been shaped, formed and sculpted, then pushed skyward and spread out across the land by a variety of human forces and environmental factors. Much of her design appears conflicted in nature by virtue of the architect's origins, ideals,

106 Molly Brown House

training, aesthetic values, style, politics and timing. Denver has become an amalgam of architectural styles built in juxtaposition to one another. The blend was born of the needs of the miners combined with the resourcefulness of the farmers and ranchers. Over the past 40 years, beginning in the early 1960s, urban developers swept through the downtown core and neighborhoods, attempting to tear down and build-out in avaricious pursuit of financial windfalls. All the while historic preservationists and community-oriented

planners have drawn battle lines in an effort to maintain the values of Denver's Western heritage—a fierce struggle that continues to this day. Each set of designers has had a hand in creating the downtown, the neighborhoods and the architectural aesthetics as they exist today.

107 Carriage on 16th Street Mall

Denver's Downtown

Imagine a place as exciting and vital as you'll find anywhere in the world—a city alive and electric where something is happening every day and night of the year. Looking for a genuinely friendly town with Western hospitality that combines the best of a world-class Big City and the Wild West? You don't have to look any further. You have arrived at the new frontier—downtown Denver. This is a proud city that readily offers her treasures. Gold miners founded Denver, and that same "can do" attitude has

108 Window view from Republic Plaza

built this place into something different and special. There are many sides to her personality—elegant, upscale, enchanting, boastful, expansive and graceful. She has shaken herself off more than once over the past century, and today she stands strong at her zenith. She is easy to get to, and easy to get around in. She offers many unique opportunities to savor the high life of entertainment, dining, shopping, conventions and the arts. She is a city rich in character and heritage. Make no mistake—downtown Denver stands center-stage among elite cities around the globe.

109 The Yearling sculpture–Denver Library

Photographing Denver

Photographing the city presents a tremendous number of lighting options and film choices—unless you are using a digital camera. A subject as demanding as the city of Denver requires an extensive shoot list, encompassing events, places and people. It is difficult to find locations like building tops, hills and porches from 360 degrees around the city to photograph from creating new and different perspectives of the skyline . Start out wide and circumnavigate the city from afar, then move in closer to capture the essence of the historic facades and architecture. Gaining height by any means is going to add perspective you might not get shooting from street level. Shooting outdoor landscape photography is best pre-dawn and at sunrise, and in the late afternoon and early evening, except for night photographs. Work to photograph people or animals outside later in the morning or later in the evening to gain contrast and control. When photographing indoors, use available light as much as possible to add a sense of realism.

Use fill flash sparingly to illuminate people, except for the occasional portrait. If you are using daylight film, a 30 percent magenta filter can balance the green cast by fluorescent lighting in night landscape photographs. One important technique in making night photographs with motion such as fireworks or streaming car lights is using the time-lapse features of your camera. Set up on a

110 Minderaser at Elitches

100

111 **Grand Finale at Union Station**

tripod to compose your photograph. Use 50 speed film with your aperture set at F8 or F11, then set your shutter speed dial to (B). As the action begins, use a cable release to depress the shutter release and hold it, counting in seconds twice the aperture setting for the exposure. If your aperture is set at F8, count 16 seconds and if at F11, count 22 seconds. You might be surprised at the amazing color you can add to your images—experiment with this technique in a number of settings. To maintain your integrity as a photographer and for all other photographers working in the field, secure permission to enter all events,

buildings and places. This is an absolute rule for photographing in the city and for your own safety wherever you photograph.

Some days you may want to plan your locations and activities to the moment; other days you may want to strike out footloose and fancy-free to find what you will on a whim. Spontaneity is an essential component in understanding the romance and attraction of city life. Either way, it is of the utmost importance that you keep your eye on the move, searching and seeking just that right moment—you must be absolutely present or the opportunity will pass you by literally "in a

112 **Denver Performing Arts Center**

flash." This is the magic and fun of photographing in the city.

Ideas for Shoots in and around Denver

Catch "The Ride" or light rail to the 16th Street Mall for images of shopping and people watching. A quick tour of downtown is not enough. A more involved study uncovers a fascinating wealth of historic architectural development. Historic structures between 50 to 130 years old are set among the new high-rises built over the past 40 years. Historic Denver, Inc. offers guided tours, and there are self-guided tours throughout downtown and the neighborhoods that have been designated historic landmarks. Downtown landmarks include Denver Art Museum, the facades along the 16th Street Mall, the spirals of Trinity Methodist Church, the Basilica of the Immaculate Conception, the Brown Palace, the Colorado State Capitol, the Daniel's and Fisher Tower, the Denver Public Library, the promenade at Civic Center Park, the Denver Mint, LoDo and Larimer Square.

There are maps to guide you on walking and driving tours. They'll lead you to giant murals painted on the walls of buidings, sculptures hung in cascading waterfalls along the bike path of Cherry Creek, tile inlaid with mosaics under overpasses on viaducts, images carved out of stags of cottonwoods in a front yard on York Street or designed into the train line between the concourses at Denver International Airport, the landmark at the Denver Design Center, the sculpture park at MCI Plaza in the Denver Tech Center, Bierstadt's painting at the top of the fifth-floor elevator at the Denver Public Library and the painted door on Santa Fe Drive.

On any given day voices of friends talking can be heard as they pass on the walking path at Wash Park. You might find a mother and daughter reading books and laughing together beside flower-filled gardens on a lazy summer's eve. Or you might hear lyrical bagpipe melodies float on the air, as if you were meeting the Highlanders of ancient Scotland—only you are in City Park. Families enjoy a holiday picnic on the Fourth of July at Sloan's Lake. Glorious flowerbeds are intricately placed and carefully manicured throughout the city. Come October, in just a few hours, volunteers clear and turn the beds in a yearly tradition of bringing the community together on behalf of parks beautification. Parks are important in the lives of Denverites

year-round. Don't overlook them as a vital part of portraying life in the city.

Don't stop at the parks though. Start at the ever-expanding Denver Zoo where there are programs for every season and every age. The Zoo is an unparalleled wildlife experience right in the heart of the city. If you get worn out photographing high-energy activities, take a tranquility break at the exquisitely landscaped Denver Botanic Gardens. Walk the desert, visit a Japanese garden or sit beside Monet's Garden, and contemplate the pure pleasure of quietude. Then come back some summer evening for a concert at the garden's outdoor amphitheatre. These are just a few of the thousands of situations in Denver waiting for you to photograph—all you need to do is take the chance to move out in it and with it.

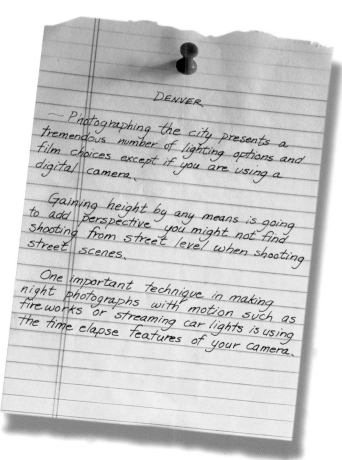

DENVER

~ Photographing the city presents a tremendous number of lighting options and film choices except if you are using a digital camera.

Gaining height by any means is going to add perspective you might not find shooting from street level when shooting street scenes.

One important technique in making night photographs with motion such as fireworks or streaming car lights is using the time elapse features of your camera.

Prairie Grasslands Reflection

THE
Northeast
AND
Southeast
REGIONS

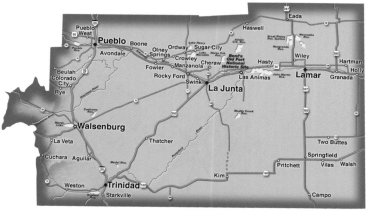

Geographically these two distinct regions are bound by lines defining their territory in Colorado. Usually places and regions are separated by their unique character, but in this case the Southeast and Northeast Regions are bound more by their similarities than their differences. However, they are distinctly different. What you see on the surface and may discover about the past of the land these regions comprise appears much the same. Both are home to extensive prairie grasslands—Pawnee National Grasslands to the north and Comanche National Grasslands to the south. Millions of years ago, both in part at one time or another were home to mountains worn flat, then covered by vast seaways leaving huge deposits of silt laid flat, ultimately shaping the high rolling plains of today. Both have vital rivers flowing through them, the Arkansas River to the south and the South

Platte and South Fork Republican Rivers in the north. Each is fed by numerous feeder streams that meander through low-lying washes and valley systems lined with cotton-woods and willows. Both are dominated by large tracks of uninhabitable arid grasslands, and both are defined by extensive fertile plains providing excellent climates for farming and ranching. Both were inhabited by Native tribes of the Great Plains—Arapaho, Sioux, Cheyenne, Ute, Apache and Comanche. Both were home to huge herds of free range bison and antelope, migratory birds such as geese, cranes, and ducks. Both played important roles in the move westward during the late 1800s with the historic Santa Fe Trail in the south and the Overland Stage Coach, and later railroad lines running from the Oregon Trail in Julesburg south to Denver. Both have histories of lawlessness. Both are prone to severe weather in the spring and summer with downpours from fast-moving storm cells and tornados. Both are born out of fire in the sky, sunrises and evenings filled with sweeping big-sky sunsets. Both were developed in the days of the Homestead Act where large tracts of land were settled almost for nothing, except for the sweat of those courageous enough to try their hand at taming them and signing a Deed of Trust. The windmill and silo set in rolling grassland hills are mirror images found in both. And both have histories filled with stories of men and women who have shaped the places we visit today. For some their abandoned prairie homes are testaments to this struggle.

Yet there are differences that separate these lands, and the people who shaped their

character and call these regions home. Distinct characteristics make each place well worth the drive to visit. The geologic icons of the Northeast set in the Pawnee National Grasslands are the formidable Pawnee Buttes. In the Southeast the beautiful Spanish Mountains northwest of Trinidad are a welcome sign to the expansive Rockies to the west. The Southeast boasts Bent's Old Fort, a National Monument near La Junta. The Southeast offers Rocky Ford cantelope and the Northeast sweet potatoes. Each has its unique and charming settlements, but none may be as inviting as Cuchara and La Veta in the Southeast. The Southeast history is linked to a strong Hispanic and Spanish tradition, going back to the 1500s—just visit the town of Aquilar. The Northeast was used as a passage south by immigrants from the Oregon Trail. Whether you find these regions similar or distinctly different, they are about life on the plains—nothing more and nothing less. This is a good draw for anyone curious enough to seek it out.

Prairie Dogs

114 Pawnee Buttes

Photographing Northeast

Pawnee Buttes

The Pawnee Buttes are an amazing set of free-standing mesas evident from miles away in the Pawnee National Grasslands. The Buttes are northeast of Ault. Take Highway 385 north to Ault, then go east on Highway 14 to New Raymer, turn left or north, then follow the signs to the Buttes. This is a remote area reached on unpaved improved roads. There is a loop that takes you by the Pawnee Buttes to Grover, then south to Briggsdale and back to Ault—be sure to have a full tank of gas before heading to these backcountry roads. It is best to spend an afternoon exploring and an evening photographing the Buttes. This is an evening or sunset shot. Work to eliminate any clutter of build out on the horizon to the east. In the spring the wildflowers are exceptional and create interest in the foreground with the Buttes in the background.

107

115 Old Prairie Farm House I

Prairie Farm House Study

Out along I-70 heading east toward Limon between Byers and Agate, there is an old prairie farmhouse that appears on the verge of collapse. It sits atop a butte overlooking a wash and old ranch land to the southwest of the frontage road that parallels the freeway. The old house and the landscape around it offer significant interest. The series of photographs shows the house from three different

116 **Old Prairie Farm House II**

angles with broken evening light and great cloud structure in the sky. A photographic study of a subject causes us to do more than work the angle we like best. It takes time to understand the composition of a specific subject before setting up and making a photograph. It might not be readily apparent what the most interesting approach to the house is. After walking around it and stopping at different places along the way to consider the options, you'll be

led to one certain perspective or possibly a number of places to view the same subject. Many times the one you were certain about doesn't hold the same value as another. You may see something in your results after reviewing your work on film or at home on the computer screen before deciding what was working and why. A study may not even lead you to a photograph that works, but going through the steps will give you insight as to how to approach the subject the next time you encounter the same thing or something similar. It could be as simple as a lens change, the length of the exposure, how you cropped the image through the lens, the type of light you selected or whether you are looking up, at, or down on the subject. With thousands of subjects to make a photographic study about, the test is how much you've learned on the way to making a study an exceptional photograph.

117 **Old Prairie Farm House III**

118 **Spanish Peaks**

Photographing Southeast

Cordova Pass

Some folks may be happy enough just to travel the Highway of Legends (a designated Colorado Scenic and Historic Byway) from Walsenberg to Trinidad via Highway 12 and see everything it has to offer geologically, historically and for sightseeing in a couple of hours. You might think otherwise, however, if you take a left turn at the top of Cuchara Pass on Forest Service Road 415 over 11,243-foot Cordova Pass. Originally known as Apishapa Pass, Corodova Pass was renamed in 1993 for a well-known local, Jose de Jesus Cordova, who loved the Spanish Peaks and

this area. Cordova Pass is the origin of the headwaters for the Apishapa River—*Apishapa* in Apache means stinking water. As the Apishapa flows out onto the plains, it pools and as it dries, it releases a strong, disagreeable smell.

There are two significant vantage points on the way over the pass. One is about three-quarters of a mile to the east from Highway 12 at the John B. Farley Memorial Overlook and a mile walk north from the parking area atop Cordova Pass. The Farley Overlook has a beautiful hillside of wildflowers blooming in summer, with the Sangre de Cristo Mountains as a backdrop to the west.

The walk from atop Cordova Pass along a ridge that runs north and south below West Spanish Peak offers an equally wonderful yet less obstructed vista for a greater length of the Sangre de Cristo Range. Both these photographs are best made at sunrise. Traveling east over the pass, you wind down a series of switchbacks through a tunnel built by the Works Progress Administration (WPA) in conjunction with the Civil Conservation Corps of Huerfano and Las Animas Counties in the early 1930s. This tunnel, an absolute work of art in stone, is a rarity because it is built through a lava dyke the road passes under. This is best photographed in the morning as the first light pierces the break in the tall trees to the east. Atop the pass Forest Road 415 merges into County Road

46.0 that carries you past Gulnare to Aguilar and I-25. About 5 miles east of the top of Cordova Pass is County Road 29.1 that turns left or north into Torrino Canyon. Follow this road for about 2.5 miles to an opening that gives you an unobstructed view of the Spanish Peaks and the lava dykes running up to it for a great evening or morning photograph.

The Highway of Legends is beautiful unto itself, but if you have the inclination, and you are not driving a motorhome, this detour is one to add to your list when visiting this area.

Great Horned Owl

111

ESSENTIALS FOR THE ROADSIDE PHOTOGRAPHER

— Have your camera equipment ready, clean and in an easy-to-find place.

— Always use a tripod, bean bag, or brace against a stable object to eliminate vibration and out-of-focus photographs.

— Carry extra batteries, film and memory (if shooting digital).

— Get directions or have a map to each location.

— Research the history, geology, wildlife, ecology, and points of interest for each location.

— Carry out what you carry in. Leave no trace.

— Walk only on designated paths.

— Do not chase wildlife or invade their habitat. We are guests in their home; treat them with respect and give them lots of room.

— Be mindful and courteous of other visitors and photographers. We must share and preserve these exquisite places as if we were the first to find them and the last to visit.

— Drive on designated roads and turn off your vehicle at all stops.

— Park in a designated, safe place and walk to your chosen location.

— Avoid photographing through car windshields or windows.

— If you must stop by the side of the road, turn off your engine and park off the road. Make sure you do not park your car on the road or halfway in the line of traffic.

— Get permission before you cross private property or from people before you take their photograph; many people are protective of their right to privacy.